# THE IRISH-AMERICAN EXPERIENCE

## A Guide To The Literature

## Seamus P. Metress

UNIVERSITY
PRESS OF
AMERICA

Library of Congress Catalog Card Number: 80-69050

83-4505

# INTRODUCTION

This work is the product of a systematic search of the literature related to the Irish-American experience. The material is scattered in a wide variety of sources such as scientific journals, dissertations, books, and popular periodicals. No attempt has been made to be selective since the value of a source is relative to the type of use one envisions for it. Therefore, all sources located are included and we leave an evaluation of their usefulness to the individual researcher.

The survey does not include material on the Irish-Americans in the Arts and Literature. It deals largely with the literature related to the fields of anthropology, economics, geography, history, political science, social psychology and sociology. It does not include the many sets of personal papers included in archival collections or the variety of government documents on immigration.

It is hoped that this work will prove to be a useful reference and research tool for those in the fields of church history, historical demography, ethnic studies, historical geography, local history, social change and urban studies. Additions to the bibliography are actively solicited by the author for inclusion in further editions and the inevitable corrections of citations are welcome.

Seamus P. Metress
Toledo, Ohio   1981

TABLE OF CONTENTS

INTRODUCTION

Chapter 1:  GENERAL WORKS ON THE IRISH IN AMERICA

Adamic, L.  1944.  Americans from Ireland.  In:
Nation of Nations.  L. Adamic.  Harper & Row, New
York, pp. 304-350.

Adams, W. F.  1932.  Ireland and Irish Emigration
to the New World from 1815 to the Famine.  Yale
Univ., New Haven, Connecticut.

Baldwin, F. S.  1901.  What Ireland has Done for
America.  New England Magazine 24:68-85.

Condon, E. O'M.  1887.  The Irish Race in America.
Ford, New York.

Considine, R. B.  1961.  It's the Irish.  Doubleday, New York.

Cross, R. D.  1978.  The Irish.  In:  Ethnic
Leadership in America.  ed. J. Higham.  Johns
Hopkins, Baltimore, pp. 176-197.

Crimmins, J. D.  1908.  Irish-American Historical
Miscellany.  John D. Crimmins, New York.

Curran, T. J.  1976.  From "Paddy" to the Presi-
dency:  The Irish in America.  In:  The Immigrant
Experience in America.  F. J. Cooper and T. J.
Curran, ed. Twayne Publ., Boston, pp. 95-114.

Desmond, H. J.  1922.  The Colonial Irish.  J.
Amer. Irish Hist. Soc. 21:165-171.

Doyle, L. F.  1948.  The Irish Calvalcade.  Catholic World, 166:522-529.

Duff, J. B.  1971.  The Irish in the United States.
Wadsworth, Belmont, California.

Fallows, M. R.  1979.  Irish Americans Identity
and Assimilation.  Prentice-Hall, Englewood Cliffs,
New Jersey.

Feagin, J. R. 1978. Irish Americans. In: Racial and Ethnic Relations. Jr. R. Feagin. Prentice-Hall, Englewood Cliffs, New Jersey, pp. 80-113.

Firkins, I. 1916. The Irish in the United States. Bulletin of Bibliography 9:22-24.

Gleason, P. 1966. Thanks to the Irish. America 114:696-699.

Grace, W. R. 1886. The Irish in America. McDonnell, Chicago.

Greeley, A. M. 1972. That Most Distressful Nation: The Taming of the American Irish. Quadrangle Books. Chicago.

Griffin, W. D. 1972. The Irish in America: A Chronology and Fact Book. Oceana, Dobbs-Ferry, New York.

Higgins, P. and F. V. Connolly. 1909. The Irish in America. John Ouseley, London.

Holiday, C. 1920. St. Patricks Folk in America. Catholic World, 110:787-95.

Hurley, D. 1939. Irish Persecutions in America. Amer. Mercury: 47:49-55.

Johnson, J. E. 1966. The Irish in America. Lerner, Minneapolis.

Kelly, J. 1884. The History of the Early Irish Settlers in America. P. J. Kenedy, New York.

Kennedy, R. E., Jr. 1976. Irish Americans: A Successful Case of Pluralism. In: The Minority Report. A. G. Dworkin and R. J. Dworkin, eds. Praeger, New York. pp. 353-372.

Lonergan, T. S. 1912. The Irish Chapter in American History. J. Amer. Irish Hist. Soc. 11: 109-121.

_____. 1912. The Irish Chapter in American History. Americana 7:502-14.

Maguire, E. 1956. The Irish in America. Hist. Bull., 35:22-30.

Maguire, J. F. 1868. The Irish in America. Longmans, Green. London. (Reprinted 1969, Arno Press).

McCaffrey, L. J. 1976. The Irish Diaspora in America. Indiana Univ., Bloomington.

McGee. T. D. 1852. A History of the Irish Settlements in North America from the Earliest Period to the Census of 1850. American Celt, Boston (Reprinted 1974. Genealogical Publ. Co., Baltimore).

_____. 1866. The Irish Position in British and Republican North America. Longmoore, Montreal.

McDonnell, V. B. 1968. The Irish Helped Build America. Messner, New York.

Miller, W. C. 1976. Irish-Americans. In: A Comprehensive Bibliography for the Study of American Minorities. New York Univ. Press. New York. Vol. I, pp. 381-422.

Moody, T. W. 1946. Irish and Scotch Irish in 18th Century America. Studies: An Irish Quarterly Rev. 35:123-140.

O'Brien, M. J. 1913. Births, Marriages and Burials and Other Records of the Irish in America in and about the 18th Century. J. Amer. Irish Hist. Soc. 12:129-175.

_____. 1915. Immigration, Land, Probate, Administration, Baptismal, Marriage, Burial, Trade, Military and Other Records of the Irish in America in the 17th and 18th Centuries. J. Amer. Irish Hist. Soc. 14:163-268.

_____. 1917. Irish Firsts in American History.
Amer. Irish Hist. Soc. Washington, D.C.

_____. 1946. Irish in America: In the 18th
Century. Catholic World, 164:58-65.

_____. ed., 1974. Irish in America. Genea-
logical Publ. Co., Baltimore, Maryland.

O'Connor, R. C. 1910. The Irish Element in
America. J. Amer. Irish Hist. Soc. 9:451-462.

O'Grady, J. P. 1973. How the Irish Became Americans. Twayne, New York.

O'Hanlon, J. 1907. Irish-American History of the
United States. 2 V. P. Murphy & Sons, New York.

O'Malley, F. W. 1929. American Sons of th' Ould
Sod. Amer. Mercury 18:25-33.

O'Sheel, S. 1932. Irish in America. Amer.
Mercury 27:501.

Potter, G. W. 1960. To the Golden Door: The
Story of the Irish in Ireland and America. Little,
Brown, Boston.

Rae, G. 1962. The Irish in America. Information,
76:16-26.

Reilly, A. J. 1945. Irish Americans. In: One
America. F. Brown & J. Roucek, eds. Prentice-Hall,
New York, pp. 43-51.

_____. 1939. Irish Americans. In: Our Racial
and National Minorities. F. Brown & J. Roucek, eds.
Prentice-Hall, New York.

Roberts, E. F. 1931. Ireland in America. G. P.
Putman's Sons, New York.

Schrier, A. 1958. Ireland and the American Emigration. University of Minnesota Press, Minneapolis, Minnesota.

Shannon, W. 1963. The American Irish. Macmillan, New York.

Sullivan, M. Y. 1910. Some Irish Contributions to Early American History. J. Amer. Irish Hist. Soc. 9:196-205.

Touhill, B. ed. 1977. Varieties of Ireland, Varieties of Irish-America. Univ. Missouri/St. Louis: St. Louis.

Wakin, E. 1976. Enter the Irish American. Crowell, New York.

Webb, R. N. 1973. America Is Also Irish. G. P. Putnam, New York.

Wibberly, L. P. 1958. The Coming of the Green. Holt, New York.

Wittke, C. 1956. The Irish in America. Louisiana State University Press. Baton Rouge, Louisiana.

_____. 1967. The Colonial Emigration from Ireland: The Irish and Scotch-Irish. In: We Who Built America. C. Wittke. Case Western Reserve, Cleveland, pp. 43-65.

_____. 1967. The Irish. In: We Who Built America. C. Wittke. Case Western Reserve, Cleveland, pp. 129-185.

_____. 1970. The Irish in America. Russell and Russell, New York (reprint).

Yetman, N. R. 1976. The Irish Experience in America. In: Irish History and Culture, H. Orel ed. Univ. of Kansas, Manhattan, pp. 247-376.

Chapter 2:   IRISH MIGRATION TO AMERICA

Abbott, E.  1926.  Historical Aspects of the Immigration Problem:  Select Documents.  Univ. of
Chicago, Chicago.

_____.  1926.  Historical Aspects of the Immi-
gration Problem:  Selected Documents.  Univ. of
Chicago, Chicago (reprint 1969 Arno Press, New York).

Adams, W. F.  1932.  Ireland and Irish Emigration
to the New World from 1815 to the Famine.  Yale
University Press, New Haven, Connecticut.

Anon.  1848.  The Irish Crises.  Edinburgh.  Rev.
138:289-97,303.

Anon.  1880.  Irish-American Colonies.  Cath. World
32:346-353.

Anon.  1918.  Emigrants in Niagra 1847.  Niagra
Hist. Soc. Publ.  31:34-41.

Anon.  1926.  Early Irish Emigrants to America
1803-1806.  Recorder 3:5:19-23.

Barry, M. J.  1863.  Irish Emigration Considered.
Cork, Ireland.

Blake, J. A.  1943.  Transportation from Ireland to
America.  Irish Historical Stud.  3:267-281.

Brady, D. S.  1964.  Relative Prices in the 19th
Century.  J. Econ. Hist.  26:145-203.

Brindley, T.  1954.  Migration and Economic Growth.
Cambridge Univ., Cambridge.

Byrne, S.  1873.  Irish Emigration to the United
States.  The Catholic Publication Society, New York
(reprinted 1969 Arno).

Carey, M.  1823.  Vindiciae Hibernicae or Ireland
Vindicated.  Carey & Lea, Philadelphia.

Coleman, T. 1972. Going to America. Pantheon Books, New York.

Condon, E. O. M. 1887. The Irish Race in America. A. E. Ford Co., New York.

Connell, K. H. 1950. The Population of Ireland 1750-1845. Claredon Press, Oxford.

Conniff, M. 1976. Strangers in a Strange Land. The Recorder 37:108-113.

Cousens, S. H. 1960. The Regional Pattern of Emigration During the Great Irish Famine 1846-51. Trans. and Papers of Instit. Brit. Geographers, No. 28.

_____. 1961. Emigration and Demographic Change in Ireland 1851-1861. Econ. Hist. Rev. 2nd Series 14:2:275-288.

Crary, C. S. 1959. The Humble Immigrant and the American Dream. Mississippi Valley Historical Review. 46:1:46-66.

Cullen, L. M. 1968. Irish History Without the Potato. Past and Present 40:72-83.

_____. 1972. An Economic History of Ireland Since 1660. Batsford, London.

Curran, T. J. 1975. Xenophobia and Immigration, 1820-1930. Twayne Press, Boston.

Curtin, M. A. 1943. Pilgrims All. Bruce, Milwaukee.

Desmond, H. J. 1900. Century of Irish Immigration. Amer. Cath. Q. Rev. 25:518-30.

_____. 1922. The Colonial Irish. J. Amer. Irish Hist. Soc. 21:165-171.

Doyle, D. 1974. American Immigrant Communities: A Critique of New England Models With Special Reference to Irish America 1890-1900. Paper. Brit. Assn. Amer. Stud. Hull England, March, 1974.

Duffy, J. 1951. The Passage to the Colonies. Mississippi Valley Historical Review. 38:1:21-38.

Dunlevy, J. A. and H. A. Gemery. 1977. British - Irish Settlement Patterns in the U.S.: The Role of Family and Friends. Scottish J. Polit. Economy. 24:257-63.

Early, C. M. 1930-31. Passengers from Ireland 1815-16. J. Amer. Irish Hist. Soc. 29:183-206.

Edwards, O. D. 1964. They Never Came Back. America. 110:336-340.

Fitzgerald, J. 1911. The Causes That Led to Irish Emigration. J. Irish Amer. Hist. Society. 10:114-123.

Flood, W. H. G. 1927. Emigration to the American Colonies, 1723 to 1773. J. Amer. Irish Hist. Soc. 26:204-206.

Fortner, R. S. 1978. The Culture of Hope and Culture of Despair: The Print Media and 19th Century Irish Emigration. Eire-Ireland, 13:3:32-48.

Freeman, T. W. 1944-45. Emigration and Rural Ireland. J. Stat. and Soc. Inquiry Soc. Ireland, 17:404-419.

_____. 1957. Pre-Famine Ireland. Manchester Univ. Manchester, England.

Gibbon, P. 1975. Colonialism and the Great Starvation in Ireland 1845-49. Race and Class 17:2: 131-139.

Gibbons, J. 1897. Irish Immigration to the United States. Irish Eccles. Rev. 4th Series, 1:97-109.

Gibson, C. 1975. The Contribution of Immigration to U.S. Population Growth. Internat. Migr. Rev. 9:2:157-177.

Grada, C. O. 1975. A Note on 19th Century Irish Immigration Statistics. Pop. Stud. 29:1:143-149.

Greenleaf, B. 1970. Flight From Famine. In: America Fever. B. Greenleaf, New American Library, New York. pp. 31-53.

Guillett, E. C. 1937. The Great Migration - The Atlantic Crossing by Sailing Ship Since 1770. Thoma, Nelson and Sons, Toronto.

Hackett, J. D. 1930. Passenger Lists Published in the Shamrock or Irish Chronicle in 1811. J. Amer. Irish Hist. Soc. 28:65-82.

Hackett, J. D. and C. M. Early. 1965. Passenger Lists from Ireland. Genealogical Publ., Baltimore.

Hale, E. E. 1852. Letters on Irish Emigration. Phillips, Sampson and Company, Boston. (report Books Librarians, 1972 Freeport, New York).

Hanock, W. N. 1873. On the Remittances from North America by Irish Emigrants considered as an indication of character of the Irish Race and with some reference to some branches of the Irish Labourers Question. J. Stat. and Social Inquiry Soc. Ireland 4:44:280-290.

Hansen, M. L. 1940. The Atlantic Migration 1607-1870. Cambridge Univ., Cambridge.

Hibernian, A. 1817. The Irish Emigrant, A Historical Tale Founded on Fact. 2 V. J. T. Sharrocks, Winchester, Virginia.

Hibernicus. 1845. What Brings So Many Irish to America. R. and E. Research Assoc. San Francisco (reprint).

Hutchinson, E. P. 1956. Immigrants and Their Children, 1850-1890. Wiley, New York.

Jones, M. A. 1960. American Immigration. Univ. of Chicago, Chicago.

Jordan, J. A. 1909. The Grosse Isle Tragedy and
the Monument to the Fever Victims 1847. Telegraph
Printing Co. Quebec.

Keep, G. R. C. 1954. Official Opinion On Irish
Emigration in the Later 19th Century. Irish Eccles.
Rev. 5th Ser. 81:6:412-421.

Kelly, M. G. 1940. Irish Catholic Colonies and
Colonization Projects in the U.S. 1795-1860.
Studies: An Irish Quart. Rev. 29:95-110, 447-
465.

Kelly, R. J. 1930. The First Irishman in America.
J. Amer. Irish Hist. Soc. 29:35-48.

Kennedy, R. E., Jr. 1973. The Irish Emigration,
Marriage and Fertility. Univ. of California,
Berkeley.

Kennedy, R. J. 1952. Single or Triple Melting
Pot. Inter-marriage in New Haven 1870-1950. Amer.
J. Sociol. 58:1:56.

Lees, L. H. and J. Modell. 1977. The Irish Coun-
trymen Urbanized: A Comparative Perspective on the
Famine Migration. J. Urban Hist. 3:4:291-308.

Lockhart, A. 1976. Some Aspects of Emigration
from Ireland to the North American Colonies Between
1660-1775. Arno Press, New York.

MacDonagh, O. 1946. Irish Emigration During the
Great Famine 1845-52. M.A. thesis. Univ. College
Dublin.

_____. 1947. The Irish Clergy and Emigration
During the Great Famine. Irish Hist. Stud. 5:20:
287-302.

_____. 1957. Irish Emigration to the United
States of America and the British Colonies During
the Famine. In The Great Famine, Studies in Irish
History 1845-52. R. D. Edwards and T. D. Williams,
eds. New York Univ., New York. pp. 319-391.

_____. 1976. The Irish Famine Emigration to the United States. Perspectives in American History, 10:357-446.

Maginis, A. J. 1892. The Atlantic Ferry, Its Ships, Men and Working. Whittaker and Co., London.

Maguire, E. G. ed. 1951. Reverend John O'Hanlon's the Irish Emigrants Guide for the United States: a critical edition with introduction and commentary. St. Louis Univ. Ph.D. dissertation. (reprinted, Arno 1969).

Maisel, A. Q. 1955. Irish Among Us. Readers Digest. 66:161-166.

Matthew, P. 1839. Emigration Fields: North America, The Cape, Australia and New Zealand. London.

Mayo-Smith, R. 1898. Emigration and Immigration. Scribners, New York.

Meehan, J. 1954. Some Features of Irish Emigration. Internat. Labor Rev. 69:2:126-139.

Meehan, T. F. 1913. New Yorks First Irish Emigrant Society. U.S. Cath. Hist. Soc. Rec. and Stud. 6:202-211.

McGee, T. D. 1851. A History of the Irish Settlers in North America from the Earliest Period to the Census of 1850. American Celt., Boston.

McNeill, W. H. 1947. The Influence of the Potato in Irish History Cornell Univ., Ph.D. dissertation.

Miller, K. A. 1977. Emigrants and Exiles: The Irish Exodus to North America from Colonial Times to the First World War. Univ. of California, Berkeley, Ph.D. dissertation.

Mooney, T. 1850. Nine Years in America. James McGlashen, Dublin.

Morehouse, F. 1928. The Irish Migration of the 'Forties. American Historical Review. 33:3:579-592.

Morrissey, P. J. 1958. Working Conditions in Ireland and Their Effect on Irish Emigration: an industrial relations study. P. J. Morrissey and Sons, New York.

O'Brien, G. 1921. The Economic History of Ireland from the Union to the Famine. Longsmans, Green, London.

_____. 1940. New Light on Emigration. Harvard Univ. Press, Cambridge.

_____. 1941. New Light on Irish Emigration. Studies: An Irish Quart. Rev. 30:17-31.

O'Brien, M. J. 1913. Births, Marriages and Other Records of the Irish in America in and about the Eighteenth Century. J. Amer. Irish Hist. Soc. 12:129-135

_____. 1914. Some Interesting Shipping Statistics of the Eighteenth Century. J. Amer. Irish Hist. Soc. 13:191-201.

_____. 1919. Earliest Irish Pioneers in America. J. Amer. Irish Hist. Soc. 18:99-204.

_____. 1919. How the descendants of Irish settlers in America were called Anglo Saxons and Scotch-Irish. Amer. Cath. Hist. Soc. 18:99-109.

_____. 1919. Irish Immigrants from English Ports in the 18th Century. J. Amer. Irish Hist. Soc. 18:208-215.

_____. 1927. The Irish in the American Colonies. J. Amer. Irish Hist. Soc. 26:21-29.

_____. 1928. Pioneers in the United States and Their Descendants. J. Amer. Irish Hist. Soc. 27:17-256.

_____. 1946. Irish in America in the 18th Century. Catholic World. 164:58-65.

O'Donnell, E. 1915. The Irish Abroad. Putnam and Sons, New York.

O'Donoghue, D. J. 1906. Geographical Distrubution of Irish Ability. Benzinger, New York.

O'Donovan, J. 1864. Immigration in the United States 1840-1860: Immigrant Interviews. Author, Pittsburgh (report 1969. Arno Press).

O'Dwyer, G. F. 1932. Irish Migrations to America, 1861-1865. J. Amer. Irish Hist. Soc. 30:118-121.

_____. 1932. Migration of Irish Laborers and Tradesmen to America. J. Amer. Irish Hist. Soc. 20:118-121.

O'Grady, J. 1930. Irish Colonization in the United States. Studies: 19:387-407.

Olson, J. S. 1979. The Irish Catholics in America. In: The Ethnic Dimension in American History. J. S. Olson. St. Martins, New York, pp. 74-88.

O'Rourke, J. 1902. History of the Great Irish Famine of 1847. Duffy and Co., Dublin.

Peters, M. 1911. Irish Builders of the American Nation. J. Amer. Irish Hist. Soc. 10:144-49.

Peyton, A. J. 1853. The Emigrants Friend: or Hints on Emigration to the United States of America addressed to the People of Ireland, Cork.

Phelan, T. P. 1935. Catholics in Colonial Days. P. J. Kenedy and Sons, New York (reprinted, Gryphon Books, Ann Arbor 1971).

Philbin, P. S. 1916. Emigration from Ireland in 18th Century. J. Amer. Irish Hist. Soc. 15:330-336.

Purcell, R. J. 1938. The Irish Emigrant Society of New York. Studies: An Irish Quart. Rev. 27:585-87.

14

_____. 1947. The Irish Immigrant, the Famine and the Irish American. The Irish Ecclesiastical Record, 5th Series, 69:849-869.

Ross, E. A. 1914. Celtic Tide. Century 87:949-955.

Salaman, R. N. 1949. The History and Social Influence of the Potato. Cambridge Univ., London.

Schrier, A. 1958. Ireland and the American Emigration, 1850-1900. Univ. of Minnesota, Minneapolis.

_____. 1970. Ireland and the American Emigration, 1850-1900. Russell and Russell, New York.

Scott, W. R. 1900. The Constitution and Finance of English, Scottish, and Irish Joint-Stock Companies of 1720. University Press, Cambridge.

Self, E. 1884. Evils Incident to Immigration. No. Amer. Rev. 138:78-88.

Shannon, J. P. 1960. The Irish Catholic Immigration. In: Roman Catholicism and the American Way of Life. T. McAvoy ed. Univ. of Notre Dame, Notre Dame, Indiana. pp. 204-210.

Smith, A. E. 1947. Colonists in Bondage: White Servitude and Convict Labor in America, 1607-1776. Univ. of North Carolina, Chapel Hill, North Carolina.

Smith, G. 1883. Why Send More Irish to America. 19th Century 13:76:913-919.

Smith, J. 1912. The Irish-American As A Citizen. New Eng. Magz. 47:257-273.

Smylie, J. H. 1963. Catholics as Immigrants. Christian Century, 80:1396-1399.

Spalding, J. L. 1880. The Religious Mission of the Irish People and Catholic Colonization. The Catholic Publ. Society, New York.

Sullivan, A. M. 1883. Why Send More Irish Out of Ireland. 19th Century, 14:77:131-144.

Taylor, P. 1971. The Distant Magnet. Harper and Row. New York.

Tucker, G. 1930. The Famine Immigration to Canada 1847. Amer. Hist. Rev. 36:533-549.

Tuke (James) Fund. 1883. Emigration from Ireland, 2nd Report. National Press Agency, London.

Walsh, L. J. 1943. Life Among the Early Irish Immigrants. Catholic World, 154:716-721.

Wannan, Bill ed. 1965. Wearing of the Green. Landsdowne, London (Ginn).

Weatherford, W. D. 1955. Pioneers of Destiny: The Romance of the Appalachin People. Vulcan Press, Birmingham, Alabama.

Wibberly, L. P. 1958. The Coming of the Green, Holt, New York.

_____. 1959. The Coming of the Green. Cath. Digest, 23:2:115-122.

_____. 1959. The Coming of the Green. Cath. Digest, 23:3:111-121.

Chapter 3:   SOCIOECONOMIC STATUS AND MOBILITY OF
THE IRISH IN AMERICA

Abell, A. I.  1949.  Origins of Catholic Social Reform in the United States.  Rev. Politics.  11:294-
309.

_____.  1952.  The Catholic Factor in Urban Wel-
fare:  The Early Period 1850-1880.  Rev. of Politics,
14:289-324.

Alba, R. D.  1974.  Assimilation Among American
Catholics.  Columbia Univ.  Ph.D. dissertation.

_____.  1976.  Social Assimilation Among Amer-
ican Catholic National-Origin Groups.  Amer. Soc.
Rev.  41:1030-46.

Alfred, W.  1971.  Ourselves Alone Irish Exiles in
Brooklyn.  The Atlantic.  227:3:53-58.

_____.  1971.  Pride and Poverty:  An Irish
Integrity.  In:  The Immigrant Experience.  T. C.
Wheeler ed. Pelican Books, Baltimore, pp. 19-33.

Anderson, G. T.  1944.  The Slavery Issue as a
Factor in Massachusetts Politics From the Compro-
mise of 1850 to the Outbreak of the Civil War.
Univ. Chicago.  Ph.D. dissertation.

Anon.  1853.  St. Nicholas and Five Points.  Putnams Magz., 1:509-512.

Appel, J. J.  1960.  The New England Origins of the
American Irish Historical Society.  New England
Quart.  33:4:462-475.

_____.  1970.  Ethnic Stereotypes in Graphic
Humor:  Paddy and Sambo.  63rd Mtg. Organiz. of
Emer. Historians.  Los Angeles, April 18, 1970.

_____.  1971.  From Shanties to Lace Cutrains:
The Irish Image in Puck, 1877-1910.  Comp. Stud.
Soc. Hist. 13:4:365-375.

Asbury, H. 1927. The Gangs of New York: An Informal History of the Underworld. Knopf.

Bagenal, Ph.D. 1882. Uncle Pat's Cabin. Nineteenth Century 12:925-938.

Bales, R. 1944. The Fixation Factor in Alcohol Addiction: A Hypothesis Derived from a Comparative Study of Irish and Jewish Norms. Harvard Univ. Ph.D. dissertation.

Banning, M. C. 1954. There's Still Hope for the Irish. Jubilee 1:7-11.

Barrett, J. P. 1970. The Life and Death of an Irish Neighborhood. Phila. Magz. 61:3:85-87, 128-263.

_____. 1975. The Sesqui-Centennial History of St. Denis Parish. St. Denis Parish, Havertown, Pennsylvania.

Barron, M. 1949. Intermediacy. Conceptualization of Irish Status in America. Social Forces, 27:256-263.

Bayor, R. H. 1978. Neighbors in Conflict. The Irish, Germans, Jews and Italians in New York City. Johns Hopkins, Baltimore.

Beadles, J. A. 1974. The Syracuse Irish 1812-1928. Immigration, Catholics, Socioeconomic Status, Politics and Irish Nationalism. Syracuse Univ., Ph.D. dissertation.

Betts, J. R. 1966. The Negro and the New England Conscience in the Days of John Boyle O'Reilly. J. Negro Hist. 51:4:246-261.

Biddle, E. H. 1976. The American Catholic Irish Family. In: Ethnic Families in America. C. M. Mindel and R. Habenstein, eds. Elsevier, New York, pp. 89-123.

Birmingham, S. 1973. Real Lace: America's Irish Rich. Harper and Row, New York.

_____. 1974. From the Banks of the Shannon to the Banks of Wall Street. U.S. Catholic 39:30-35.

Blake, J. 1966. The Americanization of Catholic Reproductive Ideals. Population Studies, 20:1:27-43.

Bland, J. 1951. Hibernian Crusade: The Story of the Catholic Total Abstinence Union of America. Catholic Univ. Press, Washington, D.C.

Blessing, P. J. 1977. West Among Strangers: Irish Migration to California 1850-1880. Univ. of California. Ph.D. dissertation.

Bloomberg, M. et al. 1971. A Census Probe into Nineteenth Century Family History: Southern Michigan 1850-1880. J. Social History 5:26-45.

Blumin. S. 1969. Mobility and Change in Ante Bellum Philadelphia. In: S. Thernstrom and R. Sennett, eds. Nineteenth Century Cities. Yale Univ., New Haven, pp. 165-208.

Bodnar, J., ed. 1937. The Ethnic Experience in Philadelphia. Bucknell Univ. Press, Lewisburg, Pennsylvania.

Brace, C. L. 1880. The Dangerous Classes of New York and Twenty Years of Work Among Them. Wynkoop, New York (report 1967 Patterson Smith, Montclair, New Jersey).

Breatnac, S. 1978. The Difference Remains. In: The San Francisco Irish. J. P. Walsh, ed. Irish Literary Historical Soc., San Francisco, pp. 143-150.

Breen, G. 1951. An Immigrant's Shenanigan's: Thirty-Three Jobs in Twenty Years. Exposition, New York.

Brinley, T. 1954. Migration and Economic Growth. Harvard Univ., Cambridge, Massachusetts.

Brown, R. H. 1974. I am of Ireland. Harper and Row, New York.

_____. 1975. I am of Ireland. The Recorder. 36:120-134.

Brown, T. N. 1968. Social Discrimination Against the Irish in the United States. Amer. Jewish Committee, New York.

Burstein, A. N. 1975. Residential Distribution and Mobility of Irish and German Immigrants in Philadelphia, 1850-1880. Univ. Pennsylvania. Ph.D. dissertation.

Butler, J. D. 1896. British Convicts Shipped to American Colonies. The Amer. Hist. Rev. 2:12-33.

Camann, H. 1868. The Charities of New York, Brooklyn and Staten Island. Hurd and Houghton, New York.

Camp, C. L., ed. 1928. An Irishman in the Gold Rush: The Journal of Thomas Kerr. California Historical Society Quarterly 7:3:205-227; 7:4:395-404.

_____. 1929. An Irishman in the Gold Rush: The Journal of Thomas Kerr. California Historical Society Quarterly 8:1:17-25; 8:2:167-182; 8:3:262-277.

Campbell, J. H. 1890. A History of the Friendly Sons of St. Patrick and of the Hibernian Society for Relief of Emigrants from Ireland. Hibernian Soc., Philadelphia.

Caper, Jr., G. M. 1938. Yellow Fever in Memphis in the 1870's. Mississippi Valley Historical Review, 24:4:483-502.

Carey, M. 1830. Miscellaneous Essays. Carey and Hart, Philadelphia.

Casey, D. J. and R. E. Rhodes 1979. Irish American Fiction. AMS Press, New York.

Casey, G. W. 1957. Vanishing Irish-American. Information. 71:29-41.

Cestello, B. D. 1956. Catholics in American Commerse and Industry. Amer. Cath. Soc. Rev. 17: 219-233.

Chambers, W. 1854. Things as They Are in America. W. and R. Chambers, London and Edinburgh.

Clancy, J. J. 1966. A Mugwump on Minorities. J. Negro Hist. 51:174-192.

Clark, D. 1971. Muted Heritage: Gaelic in an American City. Eire-Ireland 6:1:3-7.

_____. 1972. Irish-American Presence. Ethnic Philadelphia. 3:1:3-4.

_____. 1976. News from the Old Country: Irish Newspapers in Philadelphia 1820-1970. Organiz. Amer. Historian 69th Ann. Mtg. St. Louis, April 7-10, 1976.

Clayton, L. W. 1977. The Irish Peddler Boy and Old Deery Inn. Tenn. Histor. Q. 36:2:149-160.

Clinch, B. J. 1900. Anglo Saxonism and Catholic Progress. Amer. Cath. Quart. Rev. 15:723-738.

_____. 1906. Irish Names and Their Changes. Amer. Cath. Quart. 31:81-91.

Cohler, B. J. and M. A. Lieberman. 1979. Personality Change Across the Second Half of Life: Findings From a Study of Irish, Italian and Polish-American Men and Women. In: Ethnicity and Aging. D. E. Gelfand and A. J. Kutjk eds. Springer, New York, pp. 227-245.

Cole, D. B. 1963. Immigrant City: Lawrence Mass. 1845-1921. Univ. North Carolina, Chapel Hill, North Carolina.

21

_____. 1963. The Shanty Irish, 1850-1865. In: Immigrant City. D. B. Cole. Univ. of North Carolina Chapel Hill, pp. 27-41.

Considine, R. B. 1961. Its the Irish. Doubleday, Garden City, New York.

Cook, A. 1974. The Armies of the Streets. The New York Draft Riots of 1863. Univ. Kentucky, Lexington.

Cormier, R. 1968. Yesterday's Negro. Sign 47: 5-7.

Corry, J. 1977. Golden Clan. The New York Times Magazine, March 13, 1977, 16:19.

Cosgrove, J. I. 1926. The Hibernian of Charleston, South Carolina. J. Amer. Irish Hist. Soc. 25:150-158.

Costello, A. E. 1884. Our Police Protectors: History of the New York Police. New York.

_____. 1887. Our Firemen: History of the New York Fire Department. New York.

Cross, R. D. 1962. The Changing Image of the City Among American Catholics. Cath. Hist. Rev. 48:33-52.

Cuddy, E. 1976. Are the Bolsheviks Any Worse Than the Irish? Ethno-Religious Conflict in America During the 1920's. Eire 11:3:13-32.

Cullen, T. F. 1937. William Tyler (1806-49). Cath. Hist. Rev. 23:17-30.

Cullinan, E. 1970. House of Gold. Houghton-Mifflin, Boston.

Curran, T. J. 1979. The Irish Family in 19th Century Urban America: The Role of the Catholic Church. Working Papers, Series 6, No. 2. Center for Studies in American Catholicism. Univ. Notre Dame.

Curry, L. 1972. Protestant-Catholic Relations in America. D. C. Heath, Lexington.

Cusack, M. F. 1886. Advice to Irish Girls in America. Pustet, New York.

_____. 1886. From Killarney to New York or How Thade Became a Banker. Pustet, New York.

Darling, A. B. 1924. Jacksonian Democracy in Massachusetts, 1824-1848. American Historical Review 29:2:271-287.

Davis, A. and M. Haller, eds. 1973. The Peoples of Philadelphia: A History of Ethnic Groups and Lower Class Life 1790-1940. Temple Univ., Pennsylvania.

Deasy, M. 1948. The Hour of Spring, Little, Brown, Boston.

DeForest, R. W. and L. Veiller, eds. 1903. Tenement House Problem. Macmillan, New York.

Dickens, C. 1842. American Notes. MacGibbon, London.

Doerflinger, W. M. 1951. Shantymen and Shantyboys. Macmillan, New York.

Donovan, H. D. A. 1929-30. The Continuity of the Irish Idea. J. Amer. Irish Hist. Soc. 28:112-118.

Douglas, A. 1977. Studs Lonigan and the Failure of History in Mass Society. J. Amer. Stud. 29: 487-505.

Doyle, L. F. 1948. Irish Cavalcade. Cath. World. 116:522-529.

Dubnoff, S. J. 1976. The Family and Absence from Work: Irish Workers in Lowell, Massachusetts. Cotton Mill 1860. Brandeis Univ. Ph.D. dissertation.

23

Dubovik, P. N. 1975. Housing in Holyoke and its Effects on Family Life 1800-1910. Hist. J. West. Mass. 4:1:40-50.

Duis, P. 1975. The Saloon and the City. Univ. Chicago, Ph.D. dissertation.

Dunleavy, G. W. and J. E. Dunleavy. 1975. The Irish Abroad: Evidence From the O'Connor Papers. Ethnicity. 2:3:258-270.

Dunn, J. 1916. Celtic Studies and Languages. J. Amer. Irish Hist. Soc. 15:40-50.

Dunphy, J. 1946. John Fury: A Novel in Four Parts. Harper & Row, New York.

Ellis, E. 1941. Dooley's America. Knopf, New York.

Eric, S. P. 1978. Politics the Public Sector and Irish Social Mobility, San Francisco 1870-1900. West. Polit. Quart. 31:2:274-289.

Ernst, R. 1948. Economic Nativism in New York City During the 1840's. New York Hist. 29:170-186.

Evans, H. O. 1942. Iron Pioneer Henry W. Oltrer 1840-1904. E. P. Dutton, New York.

Feldberg, M. 1975. The Philadelphia Riots of 1844: A Study of Ethnic Conflict. Greenwood Press, Westport, New York.

Fitzmaurice, N. C. 1963. Historical Development of the Educational Thought of the Reverend Peter C. Yorke, 1893-1925. Univ. San Francisco, Master's thesis.

Fleming, T. J. 1961. All Good Men. Doubleday, Garden City, New York.

_____. 1974. The Good Shepherd. Doubleday, Garden City, New York.

Foik, P. J. 1920. The Beginnings of Irish Catholic Journalism in America. Cath. Hist. Rev. 5:377-381.

Forbes, H. A. and H. Lee. 1967. Massachusetts Help to Ireland During the Great Famine. Forbes House, Milton, Massachusetts.

Foster, G. G. 1849. New York in Slices: By an Experienced Carver. W. H. Graham, W. F. Burgess, New York.

French, C., ed. 1897. Biographical History of the American Irish in Chicago. Amer. Biographical Printing Co., Chicago.

Friedman, D. J. 1973. White Militancy in Boston, Lexington Books, Lexington, Massachusetts.

Froude, J. A. 1879. Romanism and the Irish Race in the United States, Part I. North American Review, 129:277:519-536.

_____. 1880. Romanism and the Irish Race in the United States Part II. North American Review, 130:278:31-50.

Gallman, R. E. 1977. Human Capital in the 80 years of the Republic: How Much Did America Owe the Rest of the World. Amer. Econ. Rev. 67:1:27-31.

Gavin, J. 1932. Irish Myth. Forum. 87:329-333.

Geffen, E. M. 1969. Violence in Philadelphia in the 1840's and 1950's. Pennsylvania Hist. 36:381-410.

Gibson, F. E. 1951. The Attitudes of the New York Irish Toward State and National Affairs, 1848-1892. Columbia Univ., New York.

Gibson, W. 1968. A Mass for the Dead. Atheneum, New York.

Gilmore, H. W. 1944. The Old New Orleans and the New: A Case for Ecology. Amer. Soc. Rev. 9:385-394.

Gladden, W. 1893-94. The Anti-Catholic Crusade. Century Magz. 47:789-795.

Glanz, R. 1966. Jew and Irish: Historic Group Relations and Immigration. Alexander Kohut Memorial Foundations, New York.

Glasco, L. A. 1973. Ethnicity and Social Structure: Irish, Germans, and Native-Born of Buffalo, New York, 1850-1860. SUNY at Buffalo, Ph.D. dissertation.

_____. 1975. The Life Cycles and Household Structures of American Ethnic Groups: Irish, German and Native-Born Whites in Buffalo, New York, 1885. J. Urban History, 1:338-364.

_____. 1977. Ethnicity and Occupation in Mid-Nineteenth Century: Irish, Germans and Native-Born Whites in Buffalo, New York. In: Immigrants in Industrial America, R. L. Ehrlich, ed., Univ. of Virginia, Charlottesville, pp. 150-175.

_____. 1977. The Life Cycles and Household Structure of American Ethnic Groups: Irish, Germans and Native-Born Whites. Buffalo, New York. 1855. In: T. K. Hareven, Family & Kin in Urban Communities 1700-1930. New Viewpoints, New York. pp. 122-143.

Gleason, P. 1978. Greeley Watching. Rev. Politics 40:528-540.

Goering, J. M. 1971. The Emergence of Ethnic Interests: A Case of Serendipity. Social Forces, 49:379-384.

Good, P. K. 1975. Irish Adjustment to American Society: Integration or Separation? A Portrait of an Irish Catholic Parrish 1863-1886. Rec. Amer. Cath. Hist. Soc., Philadelphia. 86:7-23.

26

Gordon, M. A. 1977. Studies in Irish and Irish American Thought and Behavior in Builded Age New York City. Univ. Rochester. Ph.D. dissertation.

Grattan, T. C. 1859. Civilized America. Bradbury and Evans, London.

Greeley, A. 1971. Portrait of the Neighborhood, Changing. The Critic 30:14-23.

_____. 1971. The American Irish Since the Death of Studs Lonigan. The Critic 29:27-33.

_____. 1971. The Last of the American Irish Fade Away. New York Times Magz., March 14, 1971. pp. 32-42, 53-58.

_____. 1971. Why Can't They Be Like Us? E. P. Dutton, New York.

_____. 1972. Occupational Choice Among the American Irish. Eire-Ireland 7:1:3-9.

Greeley, A. M. 1972. Political Attitudes Among White Ethnics. Public Opinion. Quart. 36:213-20.

_____. 1972. The Ethnic and Religious Origins of Young American Scientists and Engineers: A Research Note. International Mig. Rev. 6:282-89.

_____. 1973. Making It In America Ethnic Groups and Social Status. Social Policy 4:21-29.

_____. 1975. An Irish-Italian? Italian Americana 1:2:239-245.

_____. 1975. The Importance of Neighborhood. The Recorder. 36:80-87.

_____. 1976. Ethnicity, Denomination, and Inequality. Sage Publications, Beverly Hills, California.

_____. 1978. Neighborhoods. Seabury Press, Somers, Connecticut.

Greeley, A. M. and W. C. McCready. 1974. Does Ethnicity Matter? Ethnicity 1:1:91-108.

_____. 1975. The Transmission of Cultural Heritages: The Case of the Irish and Italians. In: N. Glazer and D. P. Moynihan. Ethnicity, pp. 209-235. Harvard Univ., Cambridge, Massachusetts.

_____. 1978. A Preliminary Reconnaissance Into the Persistence and Explanation of Ethnic Subcultural Drinking Patterns. Medical Anthro. 2:4:31-52.

Greeley, A. M. and P. Rossi. 1966. The Education of Catholic Americans. Aldine, Chicago.

Green, C. M. 1939. Holyoke, Massachusetts: A Case History of the Industrial Revolution in America. Archon Books, New Haven.

Greenough, C. P. 1916. The Experiences of an Irish Immigrant, 1681. Mass. Hist. Soc. Proc. 49: 99-106.

Griffen, C. and S. Griffen. 1978. Natives and Newcomers: The Ordering of Opportunity in Poughkeepsie, New York 1850-1880. Harvard Univ. Cambridge.

Groh, L. 1955. All That Fleet From No Potatoes. Ships and the Sea. 5:1,10-13, 51-52.

Groneman, C. 1973. The Bloody Ould Sixth: A Social Analysis of a Mid-Nineteenth Century New York City Working Class Community. Univ. of Rochester, Ph.D. dissertation.

_____. 1976. Five Points Revisited: A Social Analysis of a 19th Century Slum. Organiz. Amer. Historians 69th Ann. Mtg. St. Louis, April 7-10, 1976.

_____. 1977. She Earns As a Child -- She Pays As a Man: Women Workers in a Mid-Nineteenth Century New York City Community. In: Immigrants in Industrial America 1850-1920, R. L. Ehrlich, ed. Univ. of Virginia, Charlottesville, pp. 33-46.

Guinther, J. 1972. Has Anybody Here Seen Paddy? Phila. Magz. 63:3:150-163.

Gunn, T. B. 1857. The Physiology of New York Boarding Houses. Mason, New York.

Halliday, G. 1920. St. Patricks Folk in America. Catholic World 110:787-795.

Hamill, P. 1974. The Gift. Ballantine, New York.

Handlin, O. 1959. Boston's Immigrants: A Study in Acculturation. Harvard Univ., Cambridge, Massachusetts.

Hanratty, M. F. 1933. A Study of Early Irish Contributions to the Growth of St. Louis. St. Louis Univ. Master's thesis.

Hareven, T. K. and M. Vinovskis. 1975. Marital Fertility, Ethnicity and Occupation in Urban Families: An Analysis of South Boston and the South End in 1880. J. Urban History 1:293-315.

Harkness, A., Jr. 1950. Americanism and Jenkins' Ear. Mississippi Valley Historical Review 37:1: 61-90.

Harris, S. H. 1958. The Public Career of John Louis O'Sullivan. Columbia Univ. Ph.D. dissertation.

Harrison, L. V. 1934. Police Administration in Boston. Harvard, Cambridge.

Hartt, R. L. 1921. More Irish Than Ireland, New York. Independent, 106:68-69.

Headley, J. T. 1873. The Great Riots of New York 1712-1873. Bobbs-Merrill, Indianapolis (1970).

29

Hellwig, D. J. 1977. Black Attitudes Toward Irish Immigrants. Mid-Amer. 59:1:39-49.

Henthorne, M. E. 1932. The Irish Catholic Colonization Association of the United States. The Twin City Printing Co., Champaign, Illinois.

Holden, M. 1966. Ethnic Accommodation in a Historical Case. Comp. St. Soc. Hist. 8:168-180.

Hurley, D. 1939. Irish Persecutions in America. Amer. Mercury 47:49-55.

Hutchinson, E. P. 1956. Immigrants and Their Children 1850-1950. Wiley, New York.

Ibson, J. D. 1976. Will the World Break Your Heart? A Historical Analysis of the Dimensions and Consequences of Irish American Assimilation. Brandeis Univ., Ph.D. dissertation.

Janis, R. 1972. The Churches of Detroit: A Study in Urban Social Structure 1880-1940. Univ. of Michigan, Ph.D. dissertation.

_____. 1979. Ethnic Mixture and the Persistence of Cultural Pluralism in the Church Communities of Detroit, 1880-1940. Mid-America 61:2:99-115.

Jolly, E. R. 1910-11. The Irish Element in America. J. Irish Amer. Hist. Soc. 10:215-232.

Keehan, M. J. 1953. The Irish Catholic Beneficial Societies Founded Between 1818 and 1869. Catholic Univ., Ph.D. dissertation.

Keenan, C. 1956. On Being Irish in America. America 94:658-660.

_____. 1964. A Challenge to Irish-Americans. Civil Rights for Negroes. Interracial Rev. 37:102-104.

Kelleher, J. V. 1961. Irishness in America. Atlantic 208:38-40.

30

Kennedy, R. E., Jr. 1978. Selective Migration and the Acculturation of Immigrants: The Overseas Irish Family. Working Paper Series 4:1, Univ. of Notre Dame, Center for the Study of American Catholicism.

Killen, J. B. 1886. The Irish Question. Ford's Nat. Library, New York.

Kilroe, E. P. 1913. Saint Tammany and the Origin of the Society of Tammany, or Columbian Order in the City of New York. M. B. Brown, New York.

Knights, P. 1971. The Plain People of Boston, 1830-1860: A Study in City Growth. Oxford Univ., New York.

Knobel, D. T. 1976. Paddy and the Republic: Popular Images of the American Irish, 1820-1860. Northwestern Univ., Ph.D. dissertation.

Knoke, D. and R. B. Felson. 1974. Ethnic Stratification and Political Cleavage in the U.S. 1952-1968. Amer. J. Sociol. 80:3:630-642.

Koester, L. 1948. Louisville's Blood Monday - August 6, 1855. The Hist. Bull. 26:53-54, 62-64.

Kuczynski, R. R. 1901. Fecundity of the Native and Foreign Born Population in Massachusetts. Quart. J. Econ. 16:1-36 and 141-186.

Lane, R. 1967. Policing the City Boston 1822-1885. Harvard Univ. Cambridge (report 1971 Antheneum).

Lannie, V. P. and B. C. Diethorns. 1968. For the Honor and Glory of God: The Philadelphia Bible Riots of 1840. Hist. Educ. Quart. 8:44-106.

Laurie, B. 1980. Working People of Philadelphia 1800-1850. Temple Univ., Philadelphia.

Leaming, R. E. 1923. Study of a Small Group of Irish American Children. Psychological Clinic 15: 18-40.

Lee, B. L. 1943. Discontent in New York City, 1861-1865. Catholic Univ., Washington.

Leonard, H. B. 1976. Ethnic Conflict and Episcopal Power. The Diocese of Cleveland 1847-1870. Cath. Hist. Rev. 62:388-407.

Leonard, S. J. 1977. The Irish, English and Germans in Denver 1860-90. Colo. Magz. 54:2:126-153.

Lewis, A. H. 1977. Those Philadelphia Kellys: With a Touch of Grace. Morrow, New York.

Lieber, F. 1835. The Stranger in America. R. Bentley, London.

Light, D. B., Jr. 1979. Class, Ethnicity and Urban Ecology in a 19th Century City: Philadelphia Irish 1840-1890. Univ. Pennsylvania, Ph.D. dissertation.

London, H. 1967. The Irish and American Nativism in New York City 1843-47. Dublin Rev. 240:378-394.

Lonergan, T. S. 1912. The Irish Chapter in American History. J. Irish Amer. Hist. Soc. 11:109-121.

Long, J. H. 1932. A Factual Study of the Influence of Reverend P. B. Yorke on Education. Catholic Univ., Master's thesis.

Lucey, W. L. 1941. Two Irish Merchants of New England. New Eng. Quart. 14:633-645.

MacCabe, J. 1868. Secrets of the Great City. National, Philadelphia.

Manning, B. T. 1953. Irish Currents in America. Information 67:10-15.

Martin, A. 1925. The Temperance Movement in Pennsylvania Prior to the Civil War. Pa. Magz. Hist. and Biog. 49:195-200.

Martin, T. 1974. The Race That God Made Mad: A Memoir By An Architect's Granddaughter. Kansas Q. 6:2:105-114.

Marty, E. M. 1972. Ethnicity: The Skeleton of Religion in America. Church History 41:4-21.

Massey, D. 1976. Class, Racism and Bussing in Boston. Annales 8:37-49.

Mattis, M. C. 1975. The Irish Family in Buffalo, New York. 1855-75: A Sociohistorical Analysis. Washington Univ., Ph.D. dissertation.

Maynard, D. H. 1961. The World's Anti-Slavery Convention. Mississippi Valley Hist. Assoc. 47:3: 452-471.

McAvoy, T. T. 1970. Formation of the Catholic Minority. In: Catholicism in America. P. Gleason ed. Harper & Row, New York. pp. 10-27.

McCaffrey, L. J. 1929-30. The Emerald Association of Brooklyn. J. Amer. Irish Hist. Soc., 28:142-147.

_____. 1971. Pioneers of the Ghetto. Illinois Quart. 34:31-42.

_____. 1975. The Conservative Image of Irish America. Ethnicity, 2:3:271-280.

McCann, J. H. 1932. A Record of Memorials in America to Men and Women of Irish Birth. J. Amer. Irish Hist. Soc. 30:134-163.

_____. 1932. Towers of Silence Speak. J. Amer. Irish Hist. Soc. 30:134-163.

McCarthy, A. 1973. Private Faces, Public Places. Curtis Books, New York.

McCarthy, J. 1969. The Gra-a-nd Parade. Amer. Herit. 20:2:54-59,111.

McCarthy, M. 1957. Memories of a Catholic Girl-hood, Berkeley Publ. Corp., New York.

33

McCullough, L. E. 1978. Irish Music in Chicago: An Ethnomusicological Study. Univ. Pittsburgh. Ph.D. dissertation.

McGann, A. G. 1944. Nativism in Kentucky to 1860. Catholic Univ. Press, Washington.

McGinty, G. W. and E. Conly. 1976. Cullen Thomas Conly: American Irish Stowaway 1820-1876. Rushing, Shreveport, Louisiana.

McGivern, E. P. 1979. Ethnic Identity and Its Relation to Group Norms: Irish-Americans in Metropolitan Pittsburgh. Univ. of Pittsburgh. Ph.D. dissertation.

McKelvey, B. 1970. Cities as Nursuries of Self-Conscious Minorities. Pac. Hist. Rev. 37:367-381.

McKelvey, G. 1949. Rochester the Flower City, 1855-1900. Harvard, Cambridge.

McManus, T. J. 1924. A Few Outstanding Figures of Irish Ancestry at the Bench and Bar of New York. J. Amer. Irish Hist. Soc. 23:101-114.

McSorley, E. 1946. Our Own Kind. Harper, New York.

Meehan, T. F. 1913. First Irish Emigrant Society, 1819. U.S. Cath. 2:202-211.

Merwick, D. 1973. Boston Priests 1848-1910: A Study of Social and Intellectual Change. Harvard, Cambridge, Massachusetts.

Miller, D. T. 1968. Immigration and Social Stratification in Pre-Civil War New York, New York Hist. 49:157-168.

Mitchell, A. G., Jr. 1976. Irish Family Patterns in 19th Century Ireland and Lowell, Massachusetts. Boston Univ., Ph.D. dissertation.

Modell, J. and T. K. Harevan. 1973. Urbanization and the Malleable Household: An Examination of Boarding and Lodging in American Families. J. Marriage and the Family 35:467-497.

Monahan, K. 1977. The Irish Hour: An Expression of the Musical Taste and the Cultural Values of the Pittsburgh Irish Community. Ethnicity 4:1:201-215.

Morgan, J. H. 1975. The Irish of South Boston. World View 18:6:24-27.

Morgan, M. and H. H. Gordon. 1979. Immigrant Families in an Industrial City: A Study of Households in Holyoke, 1880. J. Family History 4:1: 59-68.

Moriarty, T. F. 1964. The Truth Teller and Irish Americana of the 1820's. Records. Amer. Cath. Hist. Soc. Phila. 75:39-52.

Morse, S. F. 1835. Imminent Dangers to the Free Institutions of the United States Through Foreign Immigration. Clayton, New York (report 1969, Arno).

Murphy, D. J. 1960. The Reception of Synge's Playboy in Ireland and America. 1907-1912. New York Public Library Bull. 64:515-533.

Murphy, J. J. 1954. Call For Irish American Honest Self Appraisal. Homiletic and Pastoral Rev. 54:509-13.

Murphy, R. C. and L. Mannion. 1962. The History of the Society of the Friendly Sons of St. Patrick in the City of New York, 1784-1955. Murphy and Mannion, New York.

Murray, K. 1967. Voluntary Association Among the Irish. Catholic Univ., Master's thesis.

Nam, C. B. 1959. Nationality Groups and Social Stratification in America. Social Forces 37:328-333.

Nevins, A. and M. H. Thomas eds. 1952. Diary of George Templeton Strong: The Turbulent Fifties 1850-59. Macmillan, New York.

Nicholas, T. L. 1964. Forty Years of American Life. J. Maxwell & Co., London.

Nolan, J. B. 1954. The Battle of Womelsdorf. Penna. Magz. Hist. Biog. 78:361-368.

O'Brien, M. J. 1926. Irish Schoolmasters in the American Colonies. J. Amer. Irish Hist. Soc. 25: 35-61.

_____. 1927. John McCurdy: Irish Pioneer in Connecticut. J. Amer. Irish Hist. Soc. 26:199-200.

O'Connell, Congressman. 1928. Achievements of Americans of Irish Blood in the United States. J. Amer. Irish Hist. Soc. 27:381-396.

O'Connor, E. 1970. Edge of Sadness. Bantam, New York.

O'Dowd, W. G. 1975. The Intellectual Image of the City in Social Commentary and Urban Planning: The Irish Case. Southern Illinois Univ. Ph.D. dissertation.

O'Dwyer, G. F. 1920. The Catholic Genesis of Lowell. Sullivan Brothers, Lowell, Massachusetts.

O'Farrell, C. O. 1923. Irish Family Names Anglicized and Altered. J. Amer. Irish Hist. Soc. 22: 157-160.

O'Grady, J. P. 1973. How the Irish Became Americans. Twayne Publ., New York.

O'Kane, J. M. 1975. The Ethnic Factor in American Urban Civil Disorders. Ethnicity, 2:3:230-243.

Onahan, W. J. 1882. The Day We Celebrate. Dunn, Chicago.

Pessen, E. 1971. Did Fortunes Rise and Fall Mecurially in Antebellum America? The Tale of Two Cities: Boston and New York. J. Soc. Hist. 4:339-357.

Poland, D. S. 1973. Educational Achievement and Ethnic Group Membership. Comp. Educ. Rev. 17:362-74.

Posner, R. M. 1971. The Lord and the Drayman: James Bryce vs. Denis Kearney. California Hist. Quart. 50:3:277-284.

Powers, J. F. 1947. Prince of Darkness. Doubleday, Garden City.

_____. 1963. Morte D'Urban. Popular Library, New York.

Powers, V. E. 1976. Invisible Immigrants the Pre-Famine Irish Community in Worcester, Massachusetts from 1826 to 1860. Clark Univ. Ph.D. dissertation.

Pryor, E. T., Jr. 1972. Rhode Island Family Structure 1875 and 1960. In: Household and Family in Past Time. P. Laslett and R. Walls, eds. Cambridge Univ., Cambridge, pp. 521-589.

Purcell, R. J. 1937. Irish Cultural Contribution in Early New York. Cath. Ed. Rev. 25:449-460.

_____. 1938. Irish Cultural Contribution in Early New York. Cath. Ed. Rev. 26:28-42.

Reilly, D. 1951. Irishmen in American Science. Ave. Maria 74:167-170.

Reilly, J. 1975. The Siege Mentality of the Irish American Characters in Selected Novels and Plays, 1920-1974. Bowling Green State Univ., Bowling Green, Ohio. Master's thesis.

_____. 1976. The American Bar and the Irish Pub: A Study in Comparisons and Contrasts. J. Popular Culture 10:3:573-578.

Reynolds, F. L. 1921. The Ancient Order of Hibernians. Illinois Cath. Rev. 4:22-23.

Roche, J. J. 1907. Irish Ability in the United States. J. Amer. Irish. Hist. Soc. 7:17-32.

Rossman, K. R. 1940. The Irish in America Drama in the Mid-Nineteenth Century. New York Hist. 21: 39-53.

Rossa, M. O. 1939. My Mother and Father Were Irish. Devin Adair, New York.

Rowe, K. W. 1932. Matthew Carey: A Study in American Economic Development. Johns Hopkins Univ., Ph.D. dissertation.

_____. 1933. Matthew Carey: A Study in Economic Development. Johns-Hopkins Univ., Stud. Hist. and Polit. Sci., Series 51, No. 4, Baltimore, Maryland.

Rowley, W. E. 1971. The Irish Aristocracy of Albany, 1798-1878. New York History 52:3:275-304.

Runcie, J. 1972. Hunting the Nigs in Philadelphia: The Race Riot of 1834. Penna. Hist. 39: 187-218.

Ryan, D. P. 1979. Beyond the Ballot Box: A Social History of the Boston Irish 1845-1917. Univ. Massachusetts. Ph.D. dissertation.

Ryan, G. E. 1978. Slanties and Shiftlessness: The Immigrant Irish of Henry Thoreau. Eire-Ireland, 13:3:54-78.

Ryan, J. A. 1941. Social Doctrine in Action: A Personal History. Harper & Bros., New York.

Ryan, Monsignor John A. 1941. Ethics and Political Intervention in the Field of Social Action. Rev. of Politics 3:3:300-305.

Sandalls, K. F. 1970. An Investigation of the Differential Fertility Patterns of Irish and Italian Americans. Georgetown Univ. Master's thesis.

Schlossman, S. L. 1974. The Culture of Poverty in Ante-Bellum Social Thought. Science and Society, 38:150-166.

Scully, D. J. 1907. Irish Influence in the Life of Baltimore. J. Amer. Irish Hist. Soc. 7:69-75.

Schwartz, J. 1974. Morrisiania's Volunteer Fireman, 1848-1874: The Limits of Local Institutions in a Metropolitan Age. New York Hist. 55:2:159-178.

Smith, G. B. 1971. Footloose and Fancy Free: The Demography and Sociology of a Runaway Class in Colonial Pennsylvania, 1771-1776. Bryn Mawr. Master's paper.

Smith, H. J. 1980. From Stereotype to Acculturation, the Irish-American Heritage from Brechenridge to Farrell. Kent State Univ. Ph.D. dissertation.

Solomon, B. 1956. Ancestors and Immigrants: A Changing New England Tradition. Harvard, Cambridge.

Spofford, H. P. 1881. The Servant Girl Question. Houghton Mifflin, Boston (report 1977, Arno Press, New York).

Stegner, W. 1944. Who Persecutes Boston? Atlantic 174:45-52.

Still, B. 1941. Patterns of Mid-Nineteenth Century Urbanization in the Middle West. Miss. Valley Hist. Rev. 28:187-206.

Stivers, R. 1971. The Bachelor Group Ethic and Irish Drinking. Southern Illinois Univ., Ph.D. dissertation.

_____. 1976. A Hair of the Dog: Irish Drinking and American Stereotype. Pa. St. Univ. Press, Univ. Park, Pennsylvania.

_____. 1978. Irish Ethnicity and Alcohol Use. Medical Anthropology, 2:4:121-136.

Sullivan, M. L. 1976. Where Did all the Irish Go? The Irish in St. Louis 1900-1925. Organiz. Amer. Historian 69th Ann. Mtg. St. Louis, April 7-10, 1976.

_____. 1977. St. Louis Ethnic Neighborhoods. 1850-1930. Mo. Hist. Soc. Bull. 33:64-76.

Thernstrom, S. 1964. Poverty and Progress. Harvard Univ., Cambridge, Massachusetts.

_____. 1969. Immigrants and Wasps: Ethnic Differences in Occupational Mobility in Boston 1890-1940. In: S. Thernstrom and R. Sennett. Nineteenth-Century Cities. Yale Univ., New Haven, pp. 125-164.

_____. 1970. Irish Life in Yankee City. In: Catholicism in America. P. Gleason ed. Harper & Row, New York. pp. 58-64.

_____. 1973. The Other Bostonians: Poverty and Progress in an American Metropolis 1860-1970. Harvard, Cambridge.

Toker, F. 1970. James O'Donnell: An Irish Georgian in America. J. Soc. Arch. Historians 29:132-143.

Tsuchima, C. and A. Raymond. 1969. Responses of Irish and Italian of Two Social Classes on the Marlow-Crowne Social Desirability Scale. J. Soc. Psych. 77:215-219.

Vinyard, J. M. 1975. On the Fringe in Philadelphia. J. Urban Hist. 1:4:492-98.

Votwiler, A. T. 1926. George Croghan and the Westward Movement 1741-1782. Arthur Clark, Cleveland.

Walker, F. A. 1873. American Irish and American German. Scribner's Monthly 6:172-179.

Walling, G. 1888. Recollections of a New York Police Chief of Police. Caxton, New York.

Walsh, J. P. 1971. American-Irish: West and East. Eire-Ireland 6:2:25-32.

_____. 1973. Language Problem of Irish Immigrants at the Time of the Great Famine. St. Meinrads Essays, 12:60-73.

_____. 1975. Peter Yorke and Progressivism in California, 1908. Eire-Ireland 10:2:73-81.

Ward, D. 1963. Nineteenth Century Boston: A Study in the Role of Antecendant and Adjacent Conditions in the Spatial Aspects of Urban Growth. Univ. Wisconsin. Ph.D. dissertation.

_____. 1968. The Emergence of Central Immigrant Ghettos in American Cities 1840-1920. Ann. Amer. Assn. Geg. 58:2:343-359.

_____. 1971. Cities and Immigrants: A Geography of Change in Nineteenth Century America. Oxford Univ., New York.

Ward, L. R. 1976. Those Puritanic American Irish! Modern Age 20:1:94-100.

Ware, C. F. 1931. The Early New England Cotton Manufacture: A Study in Industrial Beginnings. Houghton Mifflin, Boston.

Warner, W. L. and L. Srole. 1945. The Social Systems of American Ethnic Groups. Yale Univ., New Haven.

_____. 1945. The Melting Pot: Seven Personal Histories. In: W. L. Warner & L. Srole. The Social Systems of American Ethnic Groups. Yale Univ., New Haven, pp. 1-29.

Weber, F. J. 1970. Irish-Born Champion of the Mexican-Americans. Calif. Hist. Soc. Quart. 49:3: 233-249.

Weisz, H. 1972. Irish-American Attitudes and the Americanization of the English-Language Parochial School. New York Hist. 53:2:157-176.

Weisz, H. R. 1968. Irish American and Italian American Educational Views and Activities, 1870-1900: A Comparison. Columbia Univ. Ph.D. dissertation. (reprinted, 1976, Arno Press).

Wessel, B. B. 1931. An Ethnic Survey of Woonsocket, Rhode Island. Univ. of Chicago, Chicago.

Wheeler, R. A. 1973. Fifth Ward Irish-Immigrant Mobility in Providence 1850-1870. Rhode Island Hist. 32:53-61.

White, A. O. 1973. Antebellum School Reform in Boston: Integrationists and Separatists. Phylon 34:203-218.

White, P. L. 1967. An Irish Immigrant Housewife on the New York Frontier. New York Hist. 48:182-188.

Wiligan, W. L. 1934. A Bibliography of the Irish-American Press, 1691-1835. Brooklyn.

Williams, H. A. 1957. History of the Hibernian Society of Baltimore, 1803-1957. Hibernian Soc. of Baltimore, Baltimore.

Wilson, J. Q. 1964. Generational and Ethnic Differences Among Career Police Officers. Amer. J. Sociol. 69:522-528.

Wittke, C. 1952. The Immigrant Theme on the American State. Miss. Valley. Hist. Rev. 39:2:211-232.

Woehrer, C. E. 1978. Cultural Pluralism in American Families the Influence of Ethnicity on Social Aspects of Aging. The Family Co-ordinator, 27:4:329-339.

Chapter 4:    IRISH-AMERICANS AND THE LABOR MOVEMENT

Abell, A. I.  1955.  Catholic Reaction to Industrial Conflict:  The Arbitral Process.  1885-1900.
Cath. Hist. Rev. 41:385-407.

Abbott, E.  1905.  The Wages of Unskilled Labor in
the United States.  1850-1900.  J. Polit. Economy
13:3:321-267.

Anon.  1913.  The Molly Maguires.  Their American
Record.  National Rev. 358:637-648.

Anon.  1943.  Hibernian.  Blackwoods Magz. 254:30-
35.

Anon.  1954.  The Roots and Prospects of McCarthyism.
Monthly Rev. 5:417-34.

Anon.  1965.  Irish Mafia.  Time Literary Supplement, February 11, 1965:106.

Anspach, M. R.  1954.  The Molly Maguires in the
Anthracite Coal Regions of Pennsylvania.  1850-1890.
Now and Then.  11:25-34.

Aurand, H. W.  1968.  The Anthracite Strike of
1887-1888.  Penna. Hist. 35:172-173.

_____.  1971.  From the Molly Maguires to the
United Mine Workers:  The Social Ecology of an
Industrial Union, 1869-1897.  Temple Univ. Press,
Philadelphia, Pennsylvania.

Barnes, C. B.  1915.  The Longshoremen.  Survey,
New York.

Barrett, T.  1969.  The Mollies were Men.  Vantage
Press, New York.

Basen, N. K.  1980.  Kate Richards O'Hare:  The
"First Lady" of American Socialism, 1901-1917.
Labor Hist. 21:2:165-199.

Beers, P. B. 1966. The Molly Maguires. Amer. Hist. Illust. 1:12-22.

Berthoff, R. 1965. The Social Order of the Anthracite Region, 1825-1902. Penna. Magz. Hist. and Biog. 89:261-291.

Betten, N. 1976. Catholic Activism and the Industrial Worker. Univ. Florida, Gainsville.

Bimba, A. 1932. The Molly Maguires. Internat. Publ., New York. (1959 reprint).

Broehl, W. G. 1964. The Molly Maguires. Harvard, Cambridge, Massachusetts.

Brooks, J. G. 1897. Impressions of the Anthracite Coal Troubles. Yale Rev. 6:306-311.

Browne, H. J. 1949. Terence V. Powderly -- and the Church -- Labor Difficulties of the Early 1880's. Cath. Hist. Rev. 32:1-27.

_____. 1949. The Catholic Church and the Knights of Labor. Catholic Univ., Washington.

Carman, H. J. et al., ed. 1940. The Path I Trod: The Autobiography of T. V. Powderly. Columbia Univ., New York.

Chalker, F. 1970. Irish Catholics in the Building of the Ocmulgee and Flint Railroad. Ga. Hist. Q. 54:507-16.

Chalmers. H. II. 1964. How the Irish Built the Erie. Bookmen, New York.

Coleman, J. W. 1936. The Molly Maguire Riots: Industrial Conflict in the Pennsylvania Coal Region. Garrett and Massie, Inc., Richmond, Virginia (report Arno Press, 1969).

Coleman, J. 1943. Men and Coal. Farrar and Rhinehart, New York.

Cronin, B. C. 1943. Father Yorke and the Labor Movement in San Francisco, 1900-1910. Catholic Univ., Washington.

Dancis, B. 1978. Social Mobility and Class Consciousness: San Francisco International Workers Association in the 1880's. J. Soc. Hist. 11:75-98.

Degler, C. N. 1952. Labor in the Economy and Politics of New York City, 1850-1960. Columbia Univ., Ph.D. dissertation.

Dewees, F. P. 1877. The Molly Maguires: The Origin, Growth and Character of the Organization. Burt Franklin, New York.

Donohoe, J. M. 1953. Catholic Benevolent Union, Catholic Univ., Washington, D.C.

Dubnoff, S. J. 1976. The Family and Absence from Work: Irish Workers in a Lowell, Massachusetts Cotton Mill, 1860. Brandeis Univ., Ph.D. Dissertation, Waltham, Massachusetts.

Ehrlich, R. L. *1977.* Immigrants in Industrial America 1850-1920. Univ. of Virginia, Charlottesville, Virginia.

Erickson, C. 1957. American Industry and the European Immigrant. Harvard Univ., Cambridge.

Ernst, R. 1948. Economic Nativism in New York City During the 1840's. New York History. 29:170-186.

Falzone, V. J. 1978. Terrence V. Powderly: Middle Class Reformer. University Press America Washington, D.C.

Fetherling, D. 1974. Mother Jones: The Miners Angel. Southern Illinois Univ., Carbondale.

Foner, P. S. and A. J. Lane. 1967. James McParlan and the Molly Maguires. Sci. and Soc. 31:77.

Gibbons, P. E. 1877. The Miners of Scranton Pennsylvania. Harpers New Monthly Mgz. 15:916-927.

Gitelman, H. 1967. The Waltham System and the Coming of the Irish. Labor History 8:227-254.

_____. 1973. No Irish Need Apply: Patterns of the Response to Ethnic Discrimination in the Labor Market. Labor History 14:56-68.

_____. 1974. Workingmen of Waltham. Johns Hopkins, Baltimore.

Gluck, E. 1929. John Mitchell, Miner, John Day, New York (reprint AMS Press).

Goarty, P. W. 1953. The Economic Thought of Monsignor John A. Ryan. Catholic Univ., Washington.

Goodrich, C. L. 1925. The Miner's Freedom: A Study of the Working Life in a Changing Industry. Marshall Jones, Boston.

Gordan, M. 1975. The Labor Boycott in New York City, 1880-1886. Labor Hist. 16:2:184-229.

_____. 1977. Irish Immigrant Culture and the Labor Boycott in New York City, 1880-1886. In: Immigrants in Industrial America, 1850-1920. R. C. Ehrlich, ed. Univ. of Virginia, Charlottesville, pp. 111-122.

Goulden, J. C. 1972. Meany. Atheneum, New York.

Gowaskie, J. M. 1968. John Mitchell: A Study in Leadership. Catholic Univ., Ph.D. dissertation.

Green, A. 1960. The Death of Mother Jones. Labor History 1:68-80.

Green, V. R. 1960. The Molly Maguire Conspiracy in the Pennsylvania Anthracite Region 1862-1879. Univ. of Rochester., Masters thesis.

Griffen, C. 1969. Workers Divided: The Effect of Craft and Ethnic Differences in Poughkeepsie, New York, 1850-1880. In: Nineteenth-Century Cities. S. Thernstrom and R. Senett, eds. Yale Univ. Press, New Haven, 49-96.

_____. 1972. Occupational Mobility in Nineteenth Century America: Problems and Possibilities. J. Soc. Hist. 5:310-330.

_____. 1977. The "Old" Immigration and Industrialization: A Case Study. In: Immigrants in Industrial America. R. L. Erhlich, ed. Univ. of Virginia, Charlottesville, pp. 176-204.

Griscom, J. 1845. The Sanitary Condition of the Laboring Population of New York. Harper, New York.

Groneman, C. 1973. The Bloody Ould Sixth: A Social Analysis of a Mid-Nineteenth Century New York Working Class Community. Univ. Rochester., Ph.D. dissertation.

_____. 1978. Working Class Immigrant Women in Mid-Nineteenth Century New York: The Irish Woman's Experience. J. Urban History 4:3:255-273.

Gudelunas, W. A., Jr. and W. G. Shade. 1976. Before the Molly Maguires: The Emergence of the Ethno-Religious Factor in the Politics of the Lower Anthracite Region. 1844-72. Arno Press. New York.

Hershberg, T. 1974. Occupation and Ethnicity in Five Nineteenth-Century Cities: A Collaborative Inquiry. Hist. Methods Newsletter 7:174-216.

Hill, J. 1975. Politics, Labor and George Meany. Commonwealth 10:2:47-49.

Hurley, J. 1959. The Irish Immigrant in the Early Labor Movement 1820-1862. Columbia Univ., Masters thesis.

Itter, W. A. 1934. Early Labor Troubles in the Schuylkill Anthracite Region. Penna. Hist. 1:28-37.

_____. 1941. Conscriptions in Pennsylvania During the Civil War. Univ. of Southern California., Masters thesis.

James E. T. 1975. T. V. Powderly: A Political Profile. Penna. Magz. Hist. Biog. 99:443-459.

Jones, M. H. 1925. Autobiography of Mother Jones, edited by M. F. Parton. Charles H. Ken, Chicago.

Kildeen, C. E. 1942. John Siney: The Pioneer of American Industrial Unionism and Industrial Government. Univ. of Wisconsin. Ph.D. dissertation.

Knight, R. E. L. 1960. Industrial Relations in the San Francisco Bay Area 1900-1918. University of California, Berkeley.

Lane, A. J. 1966. Recent Literature on the Molly Maguires. Science and Society. 30:309-19.

Laurie, B. 1971. The Working People of Philadelphia 1827-1853. Univ. of Pittsburgh. Ph.D. dissertation.

Laurie, B. et al. 1977. Immigrants and Industry. The Philadelphia Experience, 1850-1880. In: Immigrants in Industrial America 1850-1920. R. L. Ehrlich, ed. Univ. of Virginia, Charlottesville, pp. 123-150.

Lazerow, J. 1980. The Workingman's Hour: The 1886 Labor Uprising in Boston. Labor Hist. 21:2: 200-220.

Leonard, J. de L. 1940. Catholic Attitudes Toward American Labor. Columbia Univ. Ph.D. dissertation.

Lewis, A. H. 1964. Lament for the Molly Maguires. Harcourt, Brace and World, New York.

Logan, S. C. 1887. A Citys Danger and Defense: On Issues and Results of the Strikes of 1877. Scranton, Pennsylvania.

Lucy, E. W. 1882. The Molly Maguire of Pennsylvania or Ireland in America. G. Bell and Sons,
London.

Man, A. P., Jr. 1951. Labor Competition and the
New York Draft Riots of 1863. J. Negro History
36:375-405.

McCarthy, C. A. 1969. The Great Molly Maguire
Hoax: Based on Information Suppressed 90 years.
Cro-Woods Publ., Wyoming, Pennsylvania.

Miller, E. W. 1955. The Southern Anthracite
Region: A Problem Area, 1820-1952. Econ. Geog.
31:331-350.

Morris, R. B. 1965. Government and Labor in Early
America. Harper, New York.

Morse, J. T. 1877. Molly Maguire Trials. Amer.
Law Rev. 11:233-60.

Musselman, B. L. 1976. Working Class Unity and
Ethnic Division: Cincinnati Trade Unionists and
Cultural Pluralism. Cincinnati Hist. Soc. Bull.
34:1:121-143.

O'Brien, D. 1966. American Catholics and Organized
Labor in the 1930's. Cath. Hist. Rev. 52:3:323-349.

Oshinsky, D. M. 1976. Senator Joseph McCarthy and
the American Labor Movement. Univ. of Missouri,
Columbia.

Parsons, T. 1954. McCarthyism and American Social
Tensions. Yale Rev. 44:226-245.

Patterson, J. F. 1913/14. Reminiscenses of John
Maguire After Fifty Years of Mining. Publ. Hist.
Soc. Schuylkill County 4:321.

Pinkerton, A. 1877. The Molly Maguires and the
Detectives. G. W. Dillingham, New York.

Pinkowski, E. 1963. John Siney: The Miners Martyr. Sunshine Press, Philadelphia.

Powers, J. L. 1943. The Knights of Labor and the Church's Attitude on Secret Societies. Univ. of Notre Dame. Masters thesis.

Raffaele, J. F. 1964. Mary Harris Jones and the United Mine Workers. Univ. of North Carolina. Masters thesis.

Rhodes, J. F. 1910. The Molly Maguires in the Anthracite Region of Pennsylvania. Amer. Hist. Rev. 15:3:547-561.

Rodechko, J. 1973. Irish-American Society in the Pennsylvania Anthracite Region 1870-1880. In: The Ethnic Experience in Philadelphia. J. E. Bodner, ed. Bucknell Univ., Lewisberg, Pennsylvania, pp. 19-38.

Roney, F. 1931. Irish Rebel and California Labor Leader: An Autobiography. Ed. by I. B. Cross. Univ. of California Press, Berkeley.

Schlegel, M. W. 1943. The Workingman's Benevolent Association: First Union of Anthracite Miners. Penna. Hist. 10:243-267.

Schroll, A. C. 1956. Bishop John Lancaster Spalding and Quadragesimo. Anno. Amer. Benedictine Rev. 7:248-62.

Shannon, F. A. 1945. A Postmortem on the Labor-Safety-Valve Theory. Agric. Hist. 19:31-37.

Shumsky, N. L. 1976. Frank Roney's San Francisco -- His Diary: April, 1975 - March, 1976. Labor Hist. 17:2:245-264.

Steel, E. 1970. Mother Jones in the Fairmont Field 1902. J. Amer. Hist. 57:290-307.

Stroh, P. 1939. The Catholic Clergy and American Labor Disputes. Catholic Univ. Ph.D. dissertation.

Sullivan, W. A.  1948.  Philadelphia Labor.  During the Jackson Era.  Penna. Hist. 15:1-16.

_____.  1954.  The Industrial Revolution and the Factory Operatives in Pennsylvania.  Penna. Magz. Hist. & Biog.  78:476-477.

_____.  1955.  The Industrial Worker in Pennsylvania 1800-1840.  Pennsylvania Historical and Museum Commission, Harrisburg.

Swejda, G. J.  1969.  Irish Immigrants Participation in the Construction of the Erie Canal.  United States Office of Archaeology and Historic Preservation.

Thompson, E.  1932.  Mines and Plantations and the Movements of Peoples.  Amer. J. Socio. 37:603-611.

Turnback, W. M.  1950.  The Attutudes of T. V. Powderly Toward Minority Groups.  Catholic Univ. Masters thesis.

Walsh, J. P.  1973.  Father Peter Yorke of San Francisco.  Studies: An Irish Quart. Rev. 62:245: 19-34.

Ware, N. J.  1924.  The Industrial Worker 1840-1860. Houghton Mifflin, Boston.

_____.  1959.  The Industrial Worker 1840-1860. Peter Smith, Gloucester, Massachusetts (reprint edition).

Wyman, M.  1979.  Hard Rock Epic:  Western Miners and the Industrial Revolution, 1860-1910.  Univ. California, Berkeley.

Chapter 5: THE IRISH-AMERICAN IN POLITICS

Abraham, E. H. 1978. Ignatius Donnelly and the Apocalyptic Style. Minn. Hist., 46:102-111.

Ainley, L. 1949. Boston Mahatma. Prendible, Boston.

Allswang, J. M. 1971. A House for All Peoples: Ethnic Politics in Chicago, 1890-1936. Lexington Books, Boston.

Anderson, J. and R. W. May. 1952. McCarthy; the Man, the Senator, the ISM. Beacon, Boston.

Angoff, C. 1949. Curley and the Boston Irish. Amer. Mercury, 69:619-627.

Anon. 1886. Power of the Irish in American Cities. Living Age, 171:382-384.

Axelrod, A. M. 1971. Ideology and Utopia in the Work of Ignatius Donnelly. Amer. Studies, 12:47-66.

Baker, J. W. 1973. Populist Themes in the Fiction of Ignatius Donnelly. Amer. Studies, 4:2:65-83.

Barry, C. J. 1958. Some Roots of American Nativism. Cath. Hist. Rev., 44:137-146.

Beals, C. 1960. Brass-Knuckle Crusade - The Great Know-Nothing Conspiracy, 1800-1860. Hasting House, New York.

Bean, W. G. 1924. An Aspect of Know-Nothingism -- The Immigrant and Slavery. South Atlantic Quart. 23:319-334.

_____. 1934. Puritan Versus Celt, 1850-1860. New England Quart. 7:70-89.

Bell, S. 1937. Rebel, Priest and Prophet: A Biography of Edward McGlynn. Devin-Adair, New York.

Berger, M. 1946. Irish Emigrant and American Nativism as Seen by British Visitors, 1836-1860. Dublin Rev., 219:174-186.

_____. 1946. Irish Emigrant and American Nativism as Seen by British Visitors, 1836-1860. Pa. Magz. Hist. Biog. 70:146-160.

Berry, B. J. L. 1973. The Human Consequences of Urbanization. Divergent Paths in the Urban Experience of the 20th Century. S. T. Martins, New York.

Beschloss, M. R. 1980. Kennedy and Roosevelt: The Uneasy Alliance. Norton, New York.

Betts, J. R. 1967. John Boyle O'Reilly and the American Paidena. Eire/Ireland, 2:4:26-52.

Billington, R. A. 1938. The Protestant Crusade, 1800-1860. Macmillan, New York.

Bishop, J. 1971. The Day Kennedy Was Shot. Funk and Wagnells, New York.

Blackmore, C. P. 1954. Joseph B. Shannon Political Boss and Twentieth Century Jeffersonian. Columbia Univ. Ph.D. dissertation.

Blodgett, G. 1966. The Gentle Reformers: Massachusetts Democrats in the Cleveland Era. Harvard, Cambridge.

Blodgett, G. T. 1962. The Mind of the Boston Mugwump. Mississippi Valley Historical Review. 48:4: 614-634.

Blum, J. M. 1951. Joe Tumulty and the Wilson Era. Houghton Mifflin, Boston.

Bocock, J. P. 1894. Irish Conquest of Our Cities. Forum, 17:186-195.

Borome, J. A. 1956. William Peter Her Majesty's Consul at Philadelphia, 1840-1843. Penna. Magz. Hist. Biog., 80:416-442.

Bradley, D. S. and M. N. Zald. 1965. From Commercial Elite to Political Administrator: The Recruitment of Mayours of Chicago. Amer. J. Socio. 71:
153-167.

Brandlee, B. C. 1975. Conversations With Kennedy.
W. W. Norton, New York.

Brauer, C. M. 1979. John F. Kennedy and the Second
Reconstruction. Columbia Univ., New York.

Breen, M. 1889. Thirty Years of New York Politics.
The Author, New York.

Brogan, D. W. 1960. Politics in America. Harper,
New York.

_____. 1964. The Catholic Politician. In:
American Aspects, D. W. Brogan. Harper and Row,
New York, pp. 164-177.

Brown, A. T. 1958. The Politics of Reform Kansas
City Municipal Government 1925-1950. Community
Studies Inc., Kansas City.

Brown, E. G. 1970. Reagan and Reality: The Two
Californias. Praeger, New York.

Brown, S. G. 1972. Presidency on Trial: Robert
Kennedy's 1968 Campaign and Afterwards. Univ.
Hawaii, Honolulu.

Browne, P. W. 1934. Thomas Dongan: Soldier and
Statesman: Irish Catholic Governor of New York,
1683-88. Studies: An Irish Quart. Rev.,23:489-
501.

Brusher, J. S. 1951. Peter Yorke and the A.P.A.
in San Francisco. The Catholic Historical Rev.,
37:129-150.

_____. 1966. Peter C. Yorke Educator Ahead of
His Time. The Catholic Educational Rev.,44:106-119.

_____. 1973. Consecrated Thunderbolt: Father Yorke of San Francisco. Hawthorne, New Jersey.

Burkley, J. P. 1974. The New York Irish: Their View of American Foreign Policy, 1914-1921. New York Univ. Ph.D. dissertation. (reprinted 1976, Arno).

Buckley, W. F., Jr. 1960. The Unmaking of a Mayor. Viking, New York.

_____. 1970. Quotations from Chairman Bill (His) Best. Arlington House, New Rochele, New York.

Buckley, W. F., Jr. and L. B. Bozell. 1954. Mc-Carthy and His Enemies. Henry Regnery, Chicago.

Buenker, J. D. 1968. Edward F. Dunne: The Urban New Stock Democrat as Progressive. Mid-America. 50:1:3-21.

_____. 1969. Urban Liberalism and the Federal Income Tax Amendment. Penna. Hist. 36:192-215.

Buhite, R. D. 1973. Patrick J. Hurley and American Foreign Policy. Cornell Univ., Ithaca, New York.

Bullough, W. A. 1978. Chris Buckley and San Francisco: The Man and the City. In: The Irish in San Francisco. J. P. Walsh ed. Irish Liter. Hist. Soc., San Francisco. pp. 27-41.

Burchell, R. A. 1972. Did the Irish and German Voters Desert the Democrats in 1920? A Tentative Statistical Answer. J. Amer. Stud., 6:153-164.

Burner, D. 1965. The Brown Derby Campaign. New York Hist. 46:387-404.

Burns, J. M. 1960. John F. Kennedy: A Political Profile. Harcourt, Brace, New York.

Burrows, F. W. 1912. Our National Debt to Ireland. New Eng. Magz. N. S. 47:255-256.

Byrnes, J. F. 1958. All in One Lifetime. Harper, New York.

Callow, A. B. 1956. San Francisco's Blind Boss. Pacific Hist. Rev. 25:261-79.

_____. 1966. Tweed Ring. Oxford Univ., New York.

Campbell, B. C. 1975-76. Ethnicity and the 1893 Wisconsin Assembly. J. Amer. Hist. 62:74-94.

Carleton, W. G. 1949. The Popish Plot of 1928: Smith-Hoover Presidential Campaign. Forum 112:141-147.

_____. 1964. Kennedy in History: An Early Appraisal Antioch Review. 24:277-299.

Carney, F. M. and H. F. Way, Jr. 1960. Politics 1960. Wadsworth, Belmont, California.

Carroll, M. C. 1955. Behind the Lighthouse: The Australian Sojourn of John Boyle O'Reilly. Iowa Univ. Ph.D. dissertation.

Carter, E. C. 1970. A "Wild Irishman" Under Every Federalists Bed: Naturalization in Philadelphia, 1789-1806. Penna. Magz. Hist. Biog. 94:331-346.

Carter, P. A. 1963. The Campaign of 1928 Re-Examined: A Study in Political Folklore. Wis. Magz. Hist. 46:263-72.

_____. 1964. The Other Catholic Candidate: The 1928 Presidential Bid of Thomas J. Walsh. Pacific Northwest Quart. 55:i-8.

Casey, R. D. 1930. The Scripps-Howard Newspapers in the 1928 Presidential Campaign. Jour. Quart. 7:207-231.

Caughey, J. W. 1957. Their Majesties Mob. Pacific Hist. Rev. 26:217-234.

Chalmers, L. 1968. Fernando Wood - Tamany Hall. New York Hist. Soc. Quart. 52:329-402.

Clark, M. J. 1974. The Bigot Disclosed: 90 Years of Nativism. Oregon Hist. Quart. 75:109-190.

Clark, T. N. 1975. The Irish Ethnic and the Spirit of Patronage. Ethnicity, 2:4:305-359.

Clemens, C. 1948. John Boyle O'Reilly: Neglected New England Poet. Poetlore, 54:361-372.

Cohn, R. 1968. McCarthy. New Amer. Libr., New York.

Colburn, D. R. 1976. Governor Alfred E. Smith and Penal Reform. Poli. Sci. Quart. 91:315-327.

Colburn, G. A. 1978. Father Conghlin and American Foreign Policy: An Irishmans Quest for Revenge. In: The San Francisco Irish, 1850-1976. J. P. Walsh. ed. Irish Liter. and Hist. Soc., San Francisco. pp. 113-125.

Connable, A. and E. Silberfarb. 1967. Tigers of Tammany. Holt, Rhinehart & Winston, New York.

Considine, J. L. 1950. Father Yorke: Champion of Human Rights. The Ave Maria. February 18, 1950: 200-208.

Cook, F. J. 1971. Nightmare Decade: The Life and Times of Senator Joe McCarthy. Random, New York.

Cornwell, E. E., Jr. 1960. Party Absorption of Ethnic Groups: The Case of Providence, Rhode Island. Social Forces, 38:205-210.

Coughlin, C. E. 1934. Eight Lectures on Labor, Capital and Justice. Radio League of the Little Flower, Royal Oak, Michigan

Coyle, J. G. 1915. American Irish Governors of Pennsylvania. J. Amer. Irish Hist. Soc. 14:145-161.

Cox, J. M. 1946. Journey Through My Years. Simon and Schuster, New York.

Creel, G. 1947. Rebel at Large. Putnam's, New York.

Croker, R. 1892. Tammany Hall and the Democracy. North Amer. Rev. 154:225-230.

Crosby, D. 1973. Angry Catholics: Catholic Opinion of Senator Joseph R. McCarthy 1950-57. Brandeis Univ. Ph.D. dissertation.

Crosby, D. F. 1978. God, Church and Flag: Senator Joe McCarthy and the Catholic Church, 1950-57. Univ. North Carolina, Chapel Hill, North Carolina.

Cuddy, E. 1969. Irish-Americans and 1916 Election: An Episode in Immigrant Adjustment. Amer. Quart. 21:228-243.

_____. 1976. Are the Bolsheviks Any Worse Than the Irish?: Ethnic-Religious Conflict in America During the 1920's. Eire/Ireland. 11:3:13-32.

Cummings, S. 1979. A Critical Examination of the Portrayal of Catholic Immigrants in American Political Life. Ethnicity. 6:197-214.

Curley, J. M. 1957. I'd Do It Again. Prentice-Hall, Englewood Cliffs, New Jersey.

Curran, M. P. 1906. The Life of Patrick Collins. Norwood Press, Norwood, Massachusetts.

Curran, T. J. 1963. Know Nothings of New York State. Columbia Univ. Ph.D. dissertation.

Curry, R. O. 1967. The Union As It Was. A Critique of Recent Interpretations of Copperheads. Civil War. 13:25-39.

Cusak, T. E. 1974. Archbishop John Ireland and the Spanish-American War: Peacemaker or Bungler. Univ. Notre Dame. Masters thesis.

Cutler, J. H. 1962. Three Steps to the White House: The Colorful Life and Times of John F. "Honey Fitz" Fitzgerald. Bobbs-Merrill, Indianapolis.

Dahl, R. A. 1961. Who Governs? Dial, New York.

Dallas, R. and J. Ratcliffe. 1973. The Kennedy Case. Putnam, New York.

Damore, L. 1967. Cape Cod Years of John Fitzgerald Kennedy. Prentice-Hall, Englewood Cliffs, New Jersey.

Davenport, J. I. 1894. The Election and Naturalization Frauds in New York City 1860-1870. New York.

David, J. ed. 1967. A Kennedy Reader. Bobbs-Merrill, Indianapolis.

David, L. 1972. Ted Kennedy: Triumphs and Tragedies. Grosset, New York.

Davis, A. 1960. Jane Addams vs. The Ward Boss. J. Ill. St. Hist. Soc. 53:247-265.

Desmond, H. J. 1912. The A.P.A. Movement. New Century, Washington, (reprinted 1976, Arno).

DeSantis, V. 1965. American Catholics and McCarthyism. Cath. Hist. Rev. 51:1:1-30.

DesMarais, P. H. John Ireland in American Politics, 1886-1906. Georgetown Univ. Masters thesis.

Deusner, C. E. 1943. The Know-Nothing Riots in Louisville. Register of the Kentucky Historical Society, 61:122-147.

Digby, M. 1949. Horace Plunkett: Anglo-American Irishman. Blackwell, Oxford.

60

Dineen, J. 1936. Ward Eight. Harper, New York.

_____. 1949. The Purple Shamrock. Norton, New York.

Dolan, J. A. 1973. A Critical Period in American Catholicism. Rev. Politics, 35:523-36.

Donnelly, E. L. ed. 1947. That Man Curley. Donnelly, Boston.

Dorsett, L. 1965. A History of the Pendergast Machine. Univ. Missouri. Ph.D. dissertation.

_____. 1968. The Pendergast Machine. Oxford Univ., New York.

Doyle, D. 1975. American Catholics, Native Rights and National Empires: Irish-American Reaction to Expansion, 1890-1905. Univ. of Iowa. Ph.D. dissertation.

Doyle, T. F. 1942. Negro in the Irish Empire. Catholic World, 154:536-44.

Duncliffe, W. J. 1965. The Life and Times of Joseph Kennedy. Macfadden-Bartell, New York.

Dupree, A. H. and L. H. Fishell, eds. 1961. An Eyewitness Account of the New York Draft Riots, July, 1863. Mississippi Valley Historical Review, 47:3:472-479.

Egan, P. F. 1916. What An Irishman Thinks of the Irish-German Alliance. Forum 56:139-146.

Eisinger, P. K. 1978. Ethnic Political Transition in Boston, 1884-1933. Pol. Sci. Quart. 93:2:217-239.

Erie, S. P. 1975. The Development of Class and Ethnic Politics in San Francisco 1870-1910: A Critique of the Pluralist Interpretation. Univ. California. Ph.D. dissertation.

Ernst, R. 1952. The One and Only Mike Walsh. New York Hist. Soc. Quart. 36:1:43-65.

Esslinger, D. R. 1967. American, German and Irish Attitudes Toward Neutrality, 1914-17: A Study of Catholic Minorities. Cath. Hist. Rev. 53:194-228.

Fairlie, H. 1973. The Kennedy Promise: The Politics of Expectation. Doubleday, New York.

Farley, J. A. 1938. Behind the Ballots. Harcourt Brace, New York.

_____. 1948. Jim Farley's Story--The Roosevelt Years. McGraw-Hill, New York.

Farrell, J. T. 1936-1937. Archbishop Ireland and Manifest Destiny. Cath. Hist. Rev. 33:269-301.

Fee, J. L. 1976. Party Identification Among American Catholics, 1972, 1973. Ethnicity, 3:1: 53-69.

Feldberg, M. 1974. The Crowd in Philadelphia History: A Comparative Perspective. Labor History 15:323-336.

Fell, M. L. 1942. The Foundations of Nativism in American Text Books, 1783-1860. Catholic Univ., Washington, D.C.

Feuerlicht, R. S. 1972. Joe McCarthy and McCarthyism: The Hate that Haunts America. McGraw-Hill, New York.

Fine, S. F. 1979. John Murphy. The New Deal Years. Univ. of Chicago. Chicago.

Fitzsimmons, L. 1972. The Kennedy Doctrine. Random House, New York.

Flynn, E. G. 1955. I Speak My Own Piece. Masses & Midstream, New York.

Flynn, E. J. 1947. You're The Boss: New York. Viking, New York.

Flynn, G. Q. 1966. Franklin D. Roosevelt and American Catholics, 1932-36. Louisiana St. Univ. Ph.D. dissertation.

Foley, W. 1930. Patrick N. Lynch, Catholic Bishop and Confederate Statesman. Univ. Notre Dame. Ph.D. dissertation.

Ford, P. 1888. The Irish Vote in the Pending Presidential Election. North Amer. Rev. 147:185-190.

Ford, T. A. 1975. The Political Crusade Against Blaine in 1884. Mid Amer. 57:1:38-55.

Fowler, G. 1949. Beau James: The Life and Times of Jimmy Walker. Viking, New York.

Fredman, L. 1961. Broderick: A Reassessment. Pacific Hist. Rev. 30:39-46.

Friedman, D. 1973. White Militancy in Boston. Lexington Books, Lexington, Massachusetts.

Friend, R. M. 1978. Men Against McCarthy. Columbia Univ., New York.

Frisch, M. H. 1969. The Community Elite and the Emergence of Urgan Politics, Springfield, Massachu-setts, 1840-1880. In: S. Thernstrom and R. Sennett. Nineteenth-Centhry Cities. Yale Univ., New Haven, pp. 277-296.

Fry, J. B. 1885. New York and The Conscription of 1863. G. P. Putnam, New York.

Fuchs, L. H. 1957. Presidential Politics in Boston: The Irish Response to Stevenson. New Eng. Quart. 30:435-447.

_____. 1967. John F. Kennedy and American Catholicism. Meredith, New York.

Fuller, H. 1962. Year of Trial: Kennedy's Crucial Decisions. Harcourt, Brace & World, New York.

Funchion, M. F. 1975. Irish Nationalists and Chicago Politics in the 1880's. Eire/Ireland. 10:2:3-18.

Gabriel, R. A. 1969. Ethnic Voting in Primary Elections: The Irish and Italians of Providence, Rhode, Island. Bureau of Government Research, Kingston, Rhode Island.

Gardner, G. C. ed. 1962. The Quotable Mr. Kennedy. Abelard-Schuman, New York.

Garnery, W. P. 1973. The Ethnic Factor in Eire Politics 1900-1970. Univ. Pittsburgh. Ph.D. dissertation.

George, J., Jr. 1978. A Catholic Family Newspaper Views the Lincoln Administration: John Mullalys' Copperhead Weekly. Civil War History 24:112-132.

Gerson, L. 1964. The Hyphenate in Recent American Politics. Univ. of Kansas, Lawrence, Kansas.

Gibson, F. E. 1951. The Attitudes of the New York Irish Toward State and National Affairs, 1848-1892. Columbia University Press, New York.

Gitelman, H. M. 1973. No Irish Need Apply. Labor Hist., 14:1:56-68.

Gleason, B. 1970. Daley of Chicago: The Man, The Mayor, and the Limits of Conventional Politics. Simon and Schuster, New York.

Gore, L. 1954. Joe Must Go. Messner, New York.

Gosnell, H. F. 1937. Machine Politics: Chicago Model. Univ. of Chicago. Chicago.

Graham, F. 1945. Al Smith American. Putnam, New York.

Green, M. B. 1966. The Problem of Boston, Norton, New York.

Greer, J. K. 1930. The Schism in the Democratic Party and the Election of 1860. La. Hist. Quart. 13:470-79.

Grossman, R. L. ed. 1961. Let Us Begin: The First 100 Days of the Kennedy Administration. Simon and Schuster, New York.

Guerrieri, D. 1962. Catholic Thought in the Age of Jackson, 1830-1840: Equal Rights and Religious Freedom. Rec. Amer. Cath. Hist. Soc., Philadelphia 73:77-91.

Hackett, F. 1914. Irish in America. Nation. 98:662-663.

_____. 1914. Where the Irish Radical Stands. New Republic, 1:16-18.

Halberstam, D. 1968. The Unfinished Odyssey of Robert Kennedy. Random, New York.

Hand, S. B. 1965. Al Smith, Franklin D. Roosevelt and the New Deal: Some Comments on Perspective. Historian 27:366-381.

Handlin, O. 1958. Al Smith and His America. Little Brown, Boston.

Hapgood, N. and H. Moskowitz. 1927. Up From the City Streets: Alfred E. Smith, A Biographical Study in Contemporary Politics. Harcourt-Brace, New York.

Hardy, O. 1928. Was Patrick Egan A Blundering Minister? Hispanic Amer. Hist. Rev. 8:65-81.

Harlow, A. F. 1955. Martys for a Free Press. Amer. Heritage 6:6:42-47.

Harris, S. H. 1960. John Louis O'Sullivan and the Election of 1844 in New York. New York Hist. 44:278-98.

de Hart, E. L. 1886. The Extradition of Political Offenders. Law Quart. Rev. 2:177-187.

Hattery, J. W. 1967. The Presidential Election Campaigns of 1928 and 1960: A Comparison of the Christian Century and America. A. J. Church and State 9:38-50.

Heale, M. J. 1976. Harbingers of Progressivism:
Responses to the Urban Crises in New York, 1845-
1860. J. Amer. Stud. 10:17-36.

Henderson, T. M. 1973. Tammany Hall and the New
Immigrants: The Progressive Years. Univ. of
Virginia. Ph.D. dissertation. (reprinted, 1976
Arno).

Heath, J. F. 1975. Decade of Disillusionment:
The Kennedy-Johnson Years. Indiana Univ., Bloomington.

Hennessy, M. E. 1935. Four Decades of Massachusetts Politics, 1890-1935. Norwood Press, Norwood,
Massachusetts.

Herlihy, D. J. 1951. Battle Against Bigotry:
Father Yorke and the American Protective Association
in San Francisco, 1893-1897. Records. Amer. Cath.
Hist. Soc., Philadelphia. 62:95-120.

Herlihy, E. ed. 1932. Fifty Years of Boston.
Boston Tercentenary Committee, Boston.

Hernon, J. M., Jr. 1957. Irish Religious Opinion
on the American Civil War. Cath. Hist. Rev.
49:508-523.

_____. 1968. Celts, Catholics and Copperheads.
Ohio State University, Columbus, Ohio.

Hersh, B. 1972. The Education of Edward Kennedy:
A Family Biography. Morrow, New York.

Higham, J. 1952. Another Look at Nativism. Cath.
Hist. Rev. 44:147-158.

_____. 1965. Strangers in the Land: Patterns
of Nativism, 1860-1925. Atheneum, New York.

Hogan, P. E. 1947. Americanism and the Catholic
University of America. Cath. Hist. Rev. 33:158-190.

Holt, M. F. 1973. The Politics of Impatience: The Origins of Know Nothingism. J. Amer. Hist. 60:2:309-331.

Honan, W. H. 1972. Ted Kennedy: Profile of a Survivor. Quadrangle, Chicago.

Howard, J. W. 1964. Frank Murphy and the Philipine Commonwealth. Pacific Hist. Rev. 33:45-68.

_____. 1968. Mr. Justice Murphy: A Political Biography. Princeton University, Princeton, New Jersey.

Hurley, D. 1941. Medal of Honor Men of Irish Birth or Ancestry in the United States Army and Navy. J. Amer. Irish. Hist. Soc. 32:57-73.

Huthmacher, J. J. 1962. Urban Liberalism and the Age of Reform. Mississippi Valley Hist. Rev. 49:231-241.

Issel, W. 1977. Class and Ethnic Conflict in San Francisco Political History: The Reform Charter of 1898. Labor Hist. 18:341-359.

Jensen, R. 1978. Party Coalitions in America 1820's to 1970's. Working Paper Series. Series 3, No. 1. Center for the Study of American Catholicism.

Johnston, W. M. 1977. On the Outside Looking In: Irish, Italian and Black Ethnic Politics in an American City. Yale Univ. Ph.D. dissertation.

Josephson, M. and H. Josephson. 1969. Al Smith: Hero of the Cities. Houghton-Mifflin, Boston.

Joyce, P. J. 1951. Memories of Father Yorke. The Furrow. 2:689-97.

Joyce, W. L. 1974. Editors and Ethnicity: A History of the Irish-American Press, 1848-1933. Univ. of Michigan. Ph.D. dissertation.

Kaiser, R. B. 1970. R. F. K. Must Die: A History of the Robert Kennedy Assassination and Its Aftermath. Dutton, New York.

Kelley, D. B. 1963. Deep South Dilemma: The Mississippi Press in the Presidential Election of 1928. J. Miss. Hist. 25:63-92.

Kennedy, E. 1976. St. Patricks Day With Mayor Daley. Seabury Press, New York.

_____. 1978. Himself: The Life and Times of Mayor Richard J. Daley. Viking, New York.

Kennedy, J. F. 1962. To Turn the Tide. Harper, New York.

_____. 1967. The Complete Kennedy Wit. Citadel, New York (ed. Bill Adler).

Kennedy, P. W. 1964. The Know-Nothing Movement in Kentucky: Role of M. J. Spalding, Catholic Bishop of Louisville. Filson Club Hist. Quart. 38:20-30.

Kennedy, R. 1974. Times to Remember. Doubleday, Garden City, New York.

Koskoff, B. Y. 1964. Joseph P. Kennedy: A Life and Times. Prentice-Hall, Englewood Cliffs, New Jersey.

Kunth, P. F. 1947. Nativism in California. Univ. of California, Berkeley. Masters thesis.

Lamparski, R. 1970. Whatever Became of James Francis Byrnes. Crown, New York.

Lane, R. 1960. James Jeffrey Roche and the Boston Pilot. New England Quart. 33:341-343.

_____. 1967. Policing the City: Boston, 1822-1885. Harvard, Cambridge, Massachusetts.

Lapomarda, V. 1970. Maurice Joseph Tobin: The Decline of Bossism in Boston. New England Quart. 43:365-366.

Large, D. 1958. An Irish Friend and the Civil War. Bull. Friends Hist. Assn. 98:20-39.

Lasky, V. 1963. J. F. K.: The Man and the Myth. Macmillan, New York.

_____. 1968. Robert F. Kennedy: The Man and the Myth. Trident, New York.

Latham, E. 1966. The Communist Controversy in Washington: From the New Deal to McCarthy. Harvard Univ., Cambridge, Massachusetts.

Laurie, B. 1974. Nothing on Impulse: Life Styles of Philadelphia Artisans, 1820-1850. Labor History. 15:335-336.

Leary, W. M., Jr. 1967. Woodrow Wilson, Irish-Americans and the Elections of 1916. J. Amer. Hist. 54:57-72.

Lens, S. 1975. Mayor Daley's Last Hurrah. The Progressive. 39:4:13-18.

Leo, E. 1931. Father Yorke in the Pulpit. The Moraga Quart. 2:30-40.

Levin, M. B. 1966. Kennedy Campaigning: The System and the Style as Practiced by Senator Edward Kennedy. Beacon, Boston.

Levine, E. M. 1966. The Irish and Irish Politicians: A Study of Cultural and Social Alienation. Univ. of Notre Dame, Notre Dame, Indiana.

Lewinson, E. R. 1965. John Purroy Mitchel: The Boy Mayor of New York. Astra Books, New York.

Lewis, A. H. 1901. Richard Croker. Life Publ. Co. New York.

Lichtman, A. J. 1979. Prejudice and the Old Politics: The Presidential Election of 1928. Univ. North Carolina Press, Chapel Hill.

Lieberson, G. 1965. John Fitzgerald Kennedy - As We Remember Him. Macmillan, New York. (ed. Joan Meyers).

Lincoln, R. 1968. Kennedy and Johnson. Holt, Rhinehart and Winston, New York.

Litt, E. 1965. The Political Culture of Massachusetts. Harvard Univ., Cambridge, Massachusetts.

_____. 1970. Beyond Pluralism: Ethnic Politics in America. Scott, Foresman, Glencoe, Illinois.

Lofton, W. H. 1949. Northern Labor and the Negro During the Civil War. J. Negro Hist. 34:251-273.

London, H. 1968. Irish Assimilation and the American Republican Party. Dublin Review. 242:65-71.

Lotchin, R. W. 1978. John Francis Neylan: San Francisco Irish Progressive. In: The Irish in San Francisco. J. P. Walsh, ed. Irish Liter. and Hist. Soc., San Francisco. pp. 87-110.

Lowi, T. 1964. At the Pleasure of the Mayor. Free Press, Glencoe, Illinois.

Lubell, S. 1952. The Chicago Irish. In The Future of American Politics. S. Lubell. Harper, New York.

Lunt, R. D. 1965. High Ministry of Government: The Political Career of Frank Murphy. Wayne State, Detroit.

MacShane, F. 1958. The Log of James Sutherland. The American Neptune. 18:4:306-314.

Mahony, W. H. 1922. American-Irish Prominent in New Jersey State and Local Government. J. Amer. Irish Hist. Soc. 21:125-145.

Manchester, W. R. 1962. Portrait of a President: John F. Kennedy in Profile. Little, Brown, Boston.

Mandebaum, S. J. 1964. The Social Setting of Intolerance: The Know Nothings, The Red Scare and McCarthyism. Scott, Roresman, Glenview, Illinois.

Man, A. P. 1951. Labor Competition and the New York Draft Riots of 1863. J. Negro Hist. 36:4:375-405.

Mann, A. 1954. Irish Catholic Liberalism. The Spirit of 1848. In: Yankee Reformers by A. Mann. Harvard Univ., Cambridge. pp. 24-51.

Marcus, S. 1973. Father Coughlin: The Tumultuous Life of the Priest of the Little Flower. Little, Brown, Boston.

Markmann, C. L. 1973. The Buckleys: A Family Examined. Morrow, New York.

Marshall, C. C. 1927. An Open Letter to the Honorable Alfred E. Smith. Atlantic Monthly, 139:4:540-549.

Martin, R. G. and E. Plant. 1960. Front Runner, Dark Horse, Doubleday, Garden City, New York.

Matthews, J. 1974. Politics of Bussing. New Rep. 171:18:3121:9-11 (November 7, 1974).

Matusow, A. J. ed. Joseph R. McCarthy. Prentice-Hall, Englewood Cliffs, New Jersey.

Maxwell, K. R. 1967-68. Irish Americans and the Fight for Treaty Ratification. Public Opinion Quarterly. 31:620-641.

McAvoy, T. T. 1944. American Catholics and the Second World War. Univ. of Notre Dame, Notre Dame, Indiana.

McBride, P. W. 1975. Culture Clash: Immigrants and Reformers, 1880-1920. R and E Research Assoc., San Francisco.

McCague, J. 1968. The Second Rebellion. Dial Press, New York.

McCarthy, J. 1952. McCarthyism: The Fight for
America. Devin-Adair, New York.

McCarthy, P. J. 1927. Autobiographic Memoirs.
Visitor, Providence, Rhode Island.

McConville, M. St. Patrick. 1928. Political
Nativism in the State of Maryland, 1830-1860.
Catholic Univ., Washington.

McCormick, R. L. 1974. Ethno-Cultural Interpretations of Nineteenth-Century American Voting
Behavior. Pol. Sci. Quart. 89:351-77.

McCune, W. 1947. Frank Murphy. In: Nine Young
Men, W. McCune, Harper, New York. pp. 137-151.

McDonald, F. 1946. The Catholic Church and Secret
Societies in the United States. U.S. Cath. Hist.
Soc., New York.

McFarland, G. 1975. Mugwumps, Morals and Politics
1884-1920. Univ. Mass., Amherst, Massachusetts.

McGann, A. G. 1944. Nativism in Kentucky, 1860.
Catholic Univ., Washington.

McGurrin, J. 1948. Bourke Cockran: A Free Lance
in American Politics. Scribners, New York.

McHugh, G. J. 1939. Political Nativism in St.
Louis, 1840-57. St. Louis University. Masters
thesis.

Meehan, T. F. 1900. Archbishop Hughes and the
Draft Riots. United States. Cath. Hist. Soc.
Hist. Rec. and Stud. 1:171-190.

Meyer, K. 1972. The Politics of Loyalty From La
Follette to McCarthy in Wisconsin, 1918-1952. Univ.
of Wisconsin. Ph.D. dissertation.

Meyerhuber, C. I. 1974. U.S. Imperialism and Ethnic Journalism: The New Manifest Destiny as Re-
flected in Boston's Irish-American Press, 1890-1900.
Eire/Ireland. 9:4:18-29.

72

Minahan, M. C. 1935. James A. McMaster: Pioneer Catholic Journalist. Catholic Univ. Masters thesis.

Mitchell, F. D. 1968. Embattled Democracy: Missouri Democratic Politics, 1919-1932. Univ. of Missouri, Columbia.

Moore, E. A. 1956. A Catholic Runs for President: The Campaign of 1928. Ronald, New York (reprinted 1968, Peter Smith).

Morgan, J. H. 1978. Ethnoconsciousness and Political Powerlessness: Boston's Irish. Social Science 53:159-167.

Moriarty, T. F. 1958. Agitation in the United States in Behalf of Catholic Emancipation as Seen Through the Truth Teller, 1824-1830. Univ. of Notre Dame. Masters thesis.

Morley, R. 1949. Masters of Politics. Funk & Wagnall, New York. (pp. 204-214, Jimmy Walker).

Morse, S. 1835. Imminent Dangers to the Free Institutions of the United States Through Foreign Immigration. New York (reprinted 1969, Arno Press).

Moskowitz, H. 1924. Alfred E. Smith: An American Career. Seltzer, New York.

Moynihan, D. P. 1961. When the Irish Ran New York. Reporter. 24:32-34.

Mugglebee, R. 1933. Father Coughlin of the Shrine of the Little Flower. L. C. Page, Boston.

_____. 1935. Father Coughlin. Doubleday, Garden City, New York.

Mulkern, J. R. 1963. The Know-Nothing Party in Massachusetts. Boston Univ. Ph.D. dissertation.

Murphy, C. 1954. McCarthy and the Businessman. Fortune. 49:156-58, 180-94.

Myers, G. 1917. The History of Tammany Hall. Boni and Liveright, New York.

Navasky, V. S. 1971. Kennedy Justice. Antheneum, New York.

Neal, N. E. 1960. The Smith-Robinson Campaign of 1928. Arkansas Hist. Quart. 19:3-11.

Nelli, H. S. 1970. John Powers and the Italians: Politics in a Chicago Ward, 1896-1921. J. Amer. Hist. 57:67-84.

Newcomb, J. L. 1977. John F. Kennedy: An Annotated Bibliography. Scarecrow, Metuchen, New Jersey.

Nie, N. H. 1974. Political Attitudes Among American Ethnics: A Study of Perceptual Distortion. Ethnicity. 1:317-343.

Noonan, C. J. 1938. Nativism in Connecticut 1829-1860. Catholic Univ., Washington, D.C.

Nunnerley, D. 1972. President Kennedy and Britain. St. Martins, New York.

O'Brien, M. 1971. Senator Joseph McCarthy and Wisconsin: 1946-1957. Univ. Wisconsin. Ph.D. dissertation.

O'Connell, M. R. 1965. Irish Politics and Social Conflict in the Age of the American Revolution. Univ. of Pennsylvania, Philadelphia.

O'Connor, E. 1956. The Last Hurrah. Little, Brown, Boston.

O'Connor, L. 1975. Clout. Henry Regnery, Chicago.

O'Connor, R. C. 1914. David Colbert Broderick. J. Irish Amer. Hist. Soc. 13:132-162.

O'Donnell, K. P. et al. 1972. Johnny We Hardly Knew You: Memoirs of John Fitzgerald Kennedy. Little, Brown, Boston.

O'Grady, J. P. 1967. The Irish. In The Immigrants Influence on Wilsons Peace Policies. J. P. O'Grady ed. Univ. of Kentucky, Lexington. pp. 56-84.

_____. 1968. The Roman Questions in American Politics: 1885. J. Church and State. 10:3:365-377.

_____. 1969. Anthony M. Keiley (1832-1905): Virginia's Catholic Politician. Cath. Hist. Rev. 54:4:613-635.

_____. 1972. Immigrants and the Politics of Reconstruction in Richmond, Virginia. Records. Amer. Cath. Hist. Soc., Philadelphia. 83:87-101.

O'Grady, M. D. 1951. The Role of Thomas J. Walsh in Senatorial Contests, 1913-1926. Univ. of Notre Dame. Ph.D. dissertation.

O'Keane, J. 1955. Thomas J. Walsh: A Senator from Montana. M. Jones Co., Francestown, New Hampshire.

Oldham, E. M. 1958. Irish Support of the Abolitionist Movement. Boston Public Library Quart. 10:175-187.

O'Malley, F. W. 1929. American Sons of the Ould Sod. Am. Mercury, 18:25-33.

O'Neil, D. J. 1971. The Study of Irish Politics in American Universities: Some Recommendations. Institute of Government Research, University of Arizona. Tucson.

Osofsky, G. 1975. Abolitionists, Irish Immigrants and the Dilemmas of Romantic Nationalism. American Historical Review, 80:4:889-912.

Packard, H. B. 1975. From Kilkenny the Background of an Intellectual Immigrant. Eire. 10:3:106-125.

Peden, J. R. 1976. Charles O'Conor and the 1872 Presidential Election. The Recorder. 37:80-90.

Peel, R. V. 1935. The Political Clubs of New York City. New York.

Peel, R. V. and T. C. Donnelly. 1931. the 1928 Campaign: An Analysis. Smith, New York.

Peterson, P. L. 1974. Stopping Al Smith: The 1928 Democratic Primary in South Dakota. South Dakota Hist. 4:439-54.

Phelan, T. P. 1918. Charles Carroll of Carrollton, Signer of the Declaration of Independence. J. Amer. Irish Hist. Soc. 17:99-120.

Piper, R. M. n.d. The Irish in Chicago. Univ. of Chicago. Masters thesis.

Polsby, N. Towards an Explanation of McCarthyism. Political Stud. 8:250-271.

Pratt, J. W. 1933. John L. O'Sullivan and Manifest Destiny. New York History. 14:213-234.

Pringle, H. F. 1927. Alfred E. Smith: A Critical Study. Macy-Masius, New York.

_____. 1929. Up to Now: An Autobiography. Viking, New York.

Purcell, R. J. 1922. Ireland and the American Civil War. Catholic World. 115:72-84.

Rakove, M. L. 1975. Don't Make No Waves, Don't Back No Losers: An Insiders Analysis of the Daley Machine. Indiana Univ. Press, Bloomington, Indiana.

Reagan, H. D. 1966. Race as a Factor in the Presidential Election of 1928 in Alabama. Alabama Rev. 19:5-19.

Reddig, W. 1947. Tom's Town, Kansas City and the Pendergast Legend. Lippincott, New York.

Reeve, C. and A. B. Reeve. 1978. James Connolly and the United States: The Road to the 1916 Rebellion. Humanities Press, Atlantic Highlands, New Jersey.

Reid, J. P. 1977. In a Defiant Stance: The Conditions of Law in Massachusetts Bay, the Irish Comparison, and the Coming of the American Revolution. Pennsylvania State University Press. University Park, Pennsylvania.

Reuter, W. 1979. The Anatomy of Political Anglophobia in the United States 1865-1900. Mid America. 61:2:117-132.

Riach, D. C. 1976. Daniel O'Connell and American Anti Slavery. Irish Hist. Stud. 20:77:3-25.

Richardson, J. F. 1961. The History of Police Protection in New York City, 1800-1870. Univ. of Michigan. Ph.D. dissertation.

_____. 1970. The New York Police: Colonial Time to 1901. Oxford Univ. Press, New York.

Ridge, M. 1962. Ignatius Donnelly: Portrait of a Politician. Univ. of Chicago, Chicago.

Riordan, J. 1978. Garret McEnerney and the Pursuit of Success. In the Irish in San Francisco. J. P. Walsh ed. Irish Liter. and Hist. Society, San Francisco. pp. 73-84.

Riordon, W. L. 1963. Plunkitt of Tammany Hall. Dutton, New York.

Robinson, F. S. 1973. Albany's O'Connell Machine. The Washington Park Spirit Inc., New York.

Roche, J. J. 1891. Life of John Boyle O'Reilly. Mershon, New York.

Rodechko, J. P. 1967. Patrick Ford and His Search for America: A Case Study of Irish-American Journalism, 1870-1913. Univ. of Conn. Ph.D. dissertation. (reprinted, 1976, Arno).

Rogers, F. 1950. Mike Walsh: A Voice of Protest. Columbia Univ. Masters thesis.

Rogin, M. 1967. The Intellectuals and McCarthy. M.I.T. Press, Cambridge.

Rorty, J. and M. Decter. 1954. McCarthy and the Communists. Beacon, Boston.

Ross, D. 1968. Robert F. Kennedy: Apostle of Change: A Review of His Public Record. Simon and Schuster, New York.

Rovere, R. 1959. Senator Joe McCarthy. Harcourt, Brace, New York.

Roy, R. L. 1953. Apostles of Discord: A Study of Organized Bigotry and Disruption on the Fringes of Protestantism. Beacon, Boston.

Royko, M. 1971. Boss: Richard J. Daley of Chicago. New American Library, New York.

Russell, F. 1971. The Irish Exile: John Boyle O'Reilly. New England Galaxy. 13:1:35-45.

Saint Henry, M. 1936. Nativism in Pennsylvania With Particular Regard to Its Effect on Politics and Education, 1840-1860. Rec. Amer. Cath. Hist. Soc., Philadelphia. 67:5-47.

Salinger, P. et al. eds. 1968. An Honorable Profession: A Tribute to Robert F. Kennedy. Doubleday, Garden City, New York.

Schafer, J. 1952. Know-Nothingism in Wisconsin. Wis. Magz. Hist., 8:3-21.

Schlesinger, A., Jr. 1960. Kennedy or Nixon: Does It Make Any Difference? MacMillan, New York.

_____. 1965. A Thousand Days: John F. Kennedy in the White House. Premier Books, New York.

Schwartz, J. A. 1964. Al Smith in the Thirties. New York Hist. 45:310-330.

Scisco, L. D. 1901. Political Nativism in New York State. Columbia Univ., New York.

78

Senning, J. P. 1914-15. The Know Nothing Movement in Illinois. J. Ill. St. Hist. Soc. 7:9-29.

Shannon, W. V. 1967. Heir Apparent: Robert Kennedy and the Struggle for Power. Macmillan, New York.

_____. 1976. The Lasting Hurrah. The New York Times Magazine. March 14, 1976:75.

Sharrow, W. B. 1972. John Hughes and a Catholic Response to Slavery in Antebellum America. J. Negro Hist. 571:3:254-269.

Shea, J. G. 1881. The Anti-Catholic Issue in the Late Election - The Relation of Catholics to Political Parties. Amer. Cath. Quart. Rev. 6:36-50.

_____. 1887. No Actual Need of a Catholic Party in the United States. Amer. Cath. Quart. Rev. 12:705-713.

Shugg, R. 1936. Suffrage and Representation in Anti-Bellum Louisiana, La. Hist. Quart. 19:396-97.

Silva, R. 1962. Rum, Religion and Votes: 1928 Re-examined. Penna. State University, University Park, Pennsylvania.

Smith, A. E. 1927. Catholic and Patriot: Governor Smith Replies. Atlantic Monthly. 139:5:721-728.

_____. 1929. Campaign Addresses of Governor Alfred E. Smith, Democratic Candidate for President, 1928. Lyon, New York.

_____. 1929. Up to Now -- An Autobiography. Garden City Publ. Co., Garden City, New York.

Smith, E. H. 1942. Charles Carroll of Carrollton. Harvard, Cambridge, Massachusetts.

Smith, J. 1912. Irish American as a Citizen. New England Magz. (NS) 141:257-273.

Smith, M. S. 1958. The Influence of the Irish Vote in Chicago and the Elections of 1884, 1888, and 1892. Univ. of Notre Dame. Masters thesis.

Smith, T. C. 1901. Expansion After the Civil War. Pol. Sci. Quart. 16:412-436.

Smith, W. D. 1964. Alfred E. Smith and John F. Kennedy. The Religious Issue During the Presidential Campaigns of 1928 and 1960. Southern Ill. Univ. Ph.D. dissertation.

Smylie, J. H. 1960. The Roman Catholic Church, the State and Al Smith. Church Hist. 29:321-43.

Snell, J. G. 1972. Thomas D'Arcy McGee and the American Republic. Can. Rev. Amer. Stud. 3:1:33-44.

Sorensen, T. C. 1965. Kennedy. Harper & Row, New York.

_____. 1969. The Kennedy Legacy. Macmillan, New York.

Starr, K. 1978. Jerry Brown: The Governor as Zen Jesuit. In: The San Francisco Irish. J. P. Walsh, ed. Irish Liter. & Hist. Soc., San Francisco, pp. 127-140.

Stave, B. M. 1970. The New Deal and the Last Hurrah. Univ. Pittsburgh, Pittsburgh.

Steele, R. V. P. 1973. When Even Angels Wept: The Senator Joe McCarthy Affair - A Story Without a Hero. Morrow, New York.

Steinke, J. 1960. The Rise of McCarthyism. Univ. Wisconsin. Masters thesis.

Stephenson, G. M. 1922-33. Nativism in the Forties and Fifties, With Special Reference to the Mississippi Valley. Miss. Valley, Hist. Rev. 9:185-202.

Stock. L. F. 1930. Catholic Participation in the Diplomacy of the Southern Confederacy. Cath. Hist. Rev. 16:1-18.

Stoddard, L. 1931. Master of Manhattens, The Life of Richard Croker. Longmans, New York.

Stolberg, B. 1946. James F. Byrnes. Amer. Mercury. 62:263-272.

Strange, D. C. 1970. Al Smith and the Republican Party at Prayer: The Lutheran Vote - 1928. Rev. Polit. 32:347-364.

Straton, H. H. and F. M. Szasz. 1968. The Reverend John Roach Straton and the Presidential Campaign of 1928. New York State Hist. 69:200-217.

Sullivan, J. T. P. 1976. In Memoriam - James A. Farley. The Recorder. 37:141-144.

Sweeney, K. 1976. Rum, Romanism Representations and Reform: Coalition Politics in Massachusetts 1847-1853. Civil War Hist. 22:116-137.

Sylvester, H. 1947. Moon Gaffney, H. Holt and Co., New York.

Syndergaard, R. 1974. Wild Irishmen and the Alien and Sedition Acts. Eire/Ireland. 9:1:17-24.

Tanzer, L. ed. 1961. The Kennedy Circle. Luce, Washington.

Tarr, J. A. 1966. J. J. Walsh of Chicago: A Case Study in Banking and Politics 1881-1905. Bus. Hist. Rev. 40:451-466.

Thelen, D. and E. Thelen. 1966. Joe Must Go: The Movement to Recall Senator Joseph McCarthy. Wis. Magz. of Hist. 49:185-209.

Thomas E. 1936. Nativism in the Old Northwest, 1850-1860. Catholic Univ., Washington.

Thompson, R. E. and H. Myers. 1962. Robert F. Kennedy: The Brother Within. Macmillan, New York.

Trow, M. 1957. Right Wing Radicalism and Political Intolerance: A Study of Support for McCarthy in a Small New England Town. Columbia Univ. Ph.D. dissertation.

_____. 1958. Small Business, Political Intolerance and Support for McCarthy. Amer. J. Socio. 64:270-81.

Tull, C. J. 1961. Father Coughlin, The New Deal and the Election of 1936. Univ. of Notre Dame. Ph.D. dissertation.

_____. 1965. Father Coughlin and the New Deal. Syracuse Univ. Press, New York.

Tuska, B. 1925. Know Nothingism in Baltimore, 1854-1860. Cath. Hist. Rev. 11:217-251.

Vanden Heuval, W. J. and M. Gwirtzman. 1970. One His Own: Robert Kennedy, 1964-1068. Doubleday, Garden City, New York.

Walker, S. 1973. Terence V. Powderly, Labor Mayor: Workingmen's Politics in Scranton, Pennsylvania, 1870-1884. Ohio State Univ. Ph.D. dissertation.

_____. 1978. The Police and the Community Scranton, Pennsylvania, 1866-1884. American Studies. 6:1:79-90.

Wallenstein, E. 1954. McCarthyism and the Conservatives. Columbia Univ. Masters thesis.

Walsh, F. R. 1968. "The Boston Pilot": A Newspaper for the Irish Immigrant, 1929-1908. Boston Univ. Ph.D. dissertation.

Walsh, G. 1976. The Politics of Cronyism. The Recorder. 37:91-95.

Walsh, J. P. 1972. Ethnic Militancy: An Irish Catholic Prototype. Rand E. Research Associates, San Francisco.

_____. 1975. Peter Yorke and Progressivism in California, 1908. Eire. 10:2:73-80.

_____. ed. 1976. The Irish: Americas Political Class, Arno Press, New York.

_____. 1978. Machine Politics, Reform, and San Francisco. In: The Irish in San Francisco. J. P. Walsh ed., Irish Liter. and Hist. Soc. pp. 59-72.

_____. 1978. Peter C. Yorke: San Francisco's Irishman Reconsidered. In: The San Francisco Irish. J. P. Walsh ed., Irish Liter. and Hist. Soc., San Francisco. pp. 43-57.

Walsh, J. P. and T. Foley. 1974. Father Peter C. Yorke: Irish-American Leader. Studia Hibernica, 14:90-103.

Walsh, M. 1843. Sketches of the Life of Mike Walsh. New York.

Ward, L. B. 1933. Father Charles E. Coughlin. Tower Publications. Detroit.

Warner, E. S. and H. Daniel. 1956. The Happy Warrior: A Biography of My Father, Alfred E. Smith. Doubleday, Garden City, New York.

Watkins, A. V. 1969. Enough Rope. Prentice-Hall, Englewood Cliffs, New Jersey.

Watson, R. A. 1964. Religion and Politics in Mid-America: Presidential Voting in Missouri 1928 and 1960. Midcontinental Amer. Stud. J. 5:33-55.

Watterson, J. S. 1980. Thomas Burke Restless Revolutionary. Univ. Press of America, Washington, D.C.

Watts, M. S. 1910. Nathan Burke. Grosset and Dunlop, New York.

Weinbaum, P. O. 1975. Temperance, Politics and the New York City Riots of 1857. New York Hist. Soc. Quart. 59:3:246-270.

Weiss, N. J. 1968. Charles Francis Murphy, 1858-1924: Respectability and Responsibility in Tammany Politics. Smith College, Northampton, Massachusetts.

Wendt, L. and H. Kogan. 1943. Lords of the Levee. Bobbs-Merrill, Indianapolis.

_____. 1967. Bosses in Lusty Chicago. Indiana Univ., Bloomington, Indiana.

Werner, M. R. 1928. Tammany Hall. Doubleday, Doran, Garden City, New York.

White, T. H. 1961. The Making of a President, 1960. Atheneum, New York.

Whyte, J. H. 1967. Political Problems of 1850-1860. In: A History of Irish Catholicism. P. J. Cornish ed. 6 Vols., Gill, Dublin. V. 5, pp. 1-34.

Whyte, W. F. 1943. Social Organization in the Slums. Amer. Socio. Rev. 8:34-39.

Willigan, W. L. 1934. A Bibliography of the Irish American Press, 1691-1835. Fordham Univ. Ph.D. dissertation.

Wisconsin Citizens Committee. 1952. The McCarthy Record. Wis. Citizen Comm. on McCarthy's Record. Madison, Wisconsin.

Wolfinger, R. E. 1965. The Development and Persistence of Ethnic Voting. Amer. Pol. Sci. Rev. 59:896-908.

Wood, G. 1960. Massachusetts Mugwumps, New Eng. Quart. 33:435-451.

Zeiger, H. A. 1968. Robert F. Kennedy: A Biography. Meredith, Des Moines, Iowa.

Zink, H. 1930. City Bosses in the United States: A Study of Twenty Municipal Bosses. Duke Univ., Durham, North Carolina.

Zolot, H. M. 1975. The Issue of Good Government and James Michael Curley: Curley and the Boston Scene from 1897-1918. State Univ. of New York. Stoney Brook. Ph.D. dissertation.

Chapter 6:  IRISH-AMERICANS AT WAR

Anon.  1925.  Some Irish-French Officers in the
French Revolution.  Recorder. 3:12-15.

Athearn, R. G.  1949.  Thomas Francis Meagher:  An
Irish Revolutionary in America.  Univ, of Colorado,
Boulder, Colorado.

Baldwin, F. S.  1901.  What Ireland Has Done for
America?  New England Magz. N. S.  24:68-85.

Bennett, W. H.  1922.  Some Pre-Civil War Irish
Militiamen of Brooklyn New York.  J. Amer. Irish
Hist. Soc. 21:172-180.

Benz, F. E.  1950.  Commodore Barry, Navy Hero.
Dodd, Mead, New York.

Bottom, R. B.  1952.  John Mitchel (1815-1875:
Irish Patriot and Defender of the Southern Cause in
the War Between the States.  Va. Magz. Hist. 60:
326-328.

Boyle, C. A.  1959.  The Memorial to the Irish
Brigade at Gettysburg.  Irish Sword.  4:68-69.

Boyle, G. E.  1923.  The 18th (or Royal Irish)
Regiment of Foot in America 1767-1775.  Soc. Army
Hist. Res. J.  2:8:63-68.

Braxton, F.  1932.  Irish in our Revolution.  Nat.
Republic.  19:24-25.

Cahill, T. P.  1937.  Captain Jeremiah O'Brien, J.
Amer. Irish. Hist. Soc.  31:12-27.

Cavanaugh, M.  1892.  Memoirs of Gen. Thomas Francis
Meagher.  Worcester, Massachusetts.

Cohalan, D. F.  1932.  General John Sullivan.  J.
Amer. Irish Hist. Soc.  30:25-59.

Condon, W. H. 1900. Life of Major-General James Shields: Hero of Three Wars and Senator from Three States. Blakely Co., Chicago.

Conyngham, D. P. 1867 The Irish Brigade and Its Campaigns. W. A. McSorley Co., New York.

Coyle, J. G. 1914. General Michael Corcoran. J. Amer. Irish Hist. Soc. 13:109-126.

_____. 1916. Irish Militiamen in the Province of New York - 1761. J. Amer. Irish Hist. Soc. 15: 168-171.

_____. 1917. The Irish Brigade of France in the Champlain Valley, 1759. J. Amer. Irish Hist. Soc. 16:126-135.

D. M. 1953. Irish in the Seventh Cavalry. Irish Sword. 1:336-338.

Dickson, C. 1958. John Mitchel and the South. Irish Sword. 3:282-283.

Duffy, F. P. 1919. Father Duffy's Story. Doran, New York.

Eno, J. N. 1927. Irish Revolutionary Soldiers in New York State and Elsewhere. Americana. 21:361-368

Fleming, T. J. 1962. The Irish of 76. Cath. Digest. 26:57-62.

Flick, E. M. E. 1935. Chaplain Duffy at the 69th Regiment. Dolphin Press, Philadelphia.

Ford, C. 1970. Donovan of O.S.S. Little, Brown, Boston.

Galway, T. F. 1890. The Irish-American Element in the Union Army. Illustrated Catholic Family Annual 70-73.

Garland, J. L. 1951-52. Irish Soldiers of the American Confederacy. Irish Sword. 1:174-180.

_____. 1958. The Formation of Meaghers Brigade Irish Brigade. Irish Sword. 3:162-165.

_____. 1961. Some Notes on the Irish during the First Month of the American Civil War. Irish Sword. 5:23-40.

Gorman, R. 1869. Speeches of Thomas Francis Meagher. New York.

Graham, J. M. 1914. Irish Loyalty to American Institutions. J. Irish Amer. Hist. Soc. 13:127-132.

Greene, M. T. 1923. American Irish in the World War. J. Amer. Irish Host. Soc. 22:150-153.

Griffen, M. I. J. 1903. Commodore John Barry: Father of the American Navy. Philadelphia.

_____. 1909. Catholics and the American Revolution. 3V. Philadelphia.

_____. 1910. The Irish Catholics and the Revolution. Amer. Cath. Hist. Res. 6:340-342.

Haltigan, J. 1908. The Irish in the American Revolution and Their Early Influence in the Colonies. P. J. Haltigan, Washington, D.C.

Hanchett, W. 1970. Irish: Charles G. Halpine in Civil War America. Syracuse Univ., Syracuse, New York.

Hardee, W. J. 1903. Biographical Sketch of Major-General Patrick R. Cleburne. So. Hist. Soc. Papers. 31:151-163.

Harris, S. H. 1964. John L. O'Sullivan Serves the Confederacy. Civil War Hist. 10:275-290.

Hasbrouck, J. E. 1925. Some Irish Revolutionary Soldiers. Recorder. 3:9-12.

Hatch, K. 1977. Saint Patrick's Battalion: Unlikely Victims of a Mexican War. Ireland of the Welcomes. 26:2:32-35.

Hay, T. R. 1959. Pat Cleburne, Stonewall Jackson of the West. McCowat-Mercer Press, Jackson, Tennessee.

Hayes, J. D. and D. D. Maguire. 1967. Charles Graham Halpine Life and Adventures of Miles O'Reilly. New York Hist. Soc. Quart. 51:326-344.

Heffernan, J. B. 1957. Ireland's Contributions to the Navies of the American Civil War. Irish Sword. 3:81-87.

Holderith, G. L. 1932. Colonel James A. Milligan and the Chicago Irish Brigade in the Civil War. Univ. of Notre Dame. Masters thesis.

Hunt, O. B. 1976. The Irish and the American Revolution. Friendly Sons of St. Patrick. Philadelphia.

J. L. G. 1960. Awards of the Congressional Medal of Honor to Irishmen. 1861-1890. Irish Sword. 4:201-203.

Jones, P. J. 1963. Irish Brigade at Fredericksburg. Cath. Digest. 27:105-110.

_____. 1969. The Irish Brigade. R. B. Luce Publ., Washington.

Lonergan, T. S. 1913. General Thomas Francis Meagher. J. Amer. Irish Hist. Soc. 12:111-126.

Lonn, E. 1940. Foreigners in the Confederacy. Univ. North Carolina, Chapel Hill.

_____. 1951. Foreigners in the Union Army and Navy. Univ. of Louisiana, Baton Rouge, Louisiana.

Love, J. E. 1950. The Autobiography of James E. Love. Mo. Hist. Soc. Bull. 6:124-138, 400-411.

Lucey, C. 1976. Harp and Sword: 1776. Amer. Irish Found, San Francisco.

Lucey, W. L. 1960. The Diary of Joseph O'Hagen J. J. Chaplain of the Excelsior Brigade. Civil War History. 6:402-209.

Lucey, C. 1977. The Irish in the American Revolution: Ireland of the Welcomes. 26:1:37-39.

MacDonagh, M. 1917. Irish Soldiers Their Humor and Seriousness. Minn. Hist. 24:46-54.

MacNamara, W. H. 1867. The Irish Ninth in Bivuoac and Battle. Boston.

_____. 1899. History of the Ninth Regiment Massachusetts Volunteers. Boston.

Maginnis, T. H. 1913. The Irish Contribution to Americas Independence. The Doire Publ. Co., Philadelphia.

McCormick, J. F., Jr. 1969. The Irish Brigade. Civil War Times Illust. 8:36-46.

Meehan, T. F. 1919. Army Statistics of the Civil War. United States Cath. Hist. Soc. Rec. & Stud. 13:129-139.

Metzer, C. H. 1915. Some Catholic Tories During the American Revolution. Cath. Hist. Rev. 4:408-427.

Mullen, T. J. 1965. The 69th Regiment at Bull Run. Irish Sword. 7:26:2-4.

_____. 1969. The Fighting Sixty-Ninth. Eire/Ireland. 4:4:13-26.

_____. 1969. The Irish Brigades in the Union Army. Irish Sword. 9:34:50-58.

Mullen, T. J., Jr. 1966. The Hibernia Regiment of the Spanish Army. Univ. of Florida, Gainsville, Florida.

Murphy, W. S. 1954. The Irish Brigade of France at the Seige of Savannah, 1779. Ga. Hist. Quart. 38:307-321.

Murray, T. A. 1903. Irish Rhode Islanders in the American Revolution. Providence, Rhode Island.

Nugent, R. 1916. The Sixty-Ninth Regiment at Fredericksburg. J. Amer. Irish Hist. Soc. 15:191-200.

O'Brien, M. J. 1918. Some Stray Historical Tidbits of the American Revolution. J. Amer. Irish Hist. Soc. 17:121-136.

_____. 1920. A Hidden Phase of American History: Ireland's Part in America's Struggle for Liberty. Dodd, Mead & Co., New York.

_____. 1922. Captain Patrick O'Flynn, Friend of George Washington. J. Amer. Irish Hist. Soc. 21:118-120.

_____. 1922. Francis McDonnell, A Son of Erin, Captured the English Flag at Stoney Point. J. Amer. Irish Hist. Soc. 21:118-120.

_____. 1922. Major Patrick Carr and Captain Patrick McGriff, Two Gallant Officers of the Georgia Continental Line. J. Amer. Irish Hist. Soc. 21:93-96.

_____. 1922. Patrick Hogan, Schoolmaster and Revolutionary Soldier. J. Amer. Irish Hist. Soc. 21:89-92.

_____. 1922. Sargent Patrick Cavanaugh, A Brave Soldier of the Revolution. J. Amer. Irish Hist. Soc. 21:86-88.

_____. 1922. The Cumberland County, Pennsylvania Militia in the Revolution. J. Amer. Irish Hist. Soc. 21:121-124.

_____. 1922. The First Regiment of the Pennsylvania Line -- The Most Famous Body of Men in the Continental Army. J. Amer. Irish Host. Soc. 21: 111-117.

_____. 1922. The Patricks and Pats of the American Revolution. J. Amer. Irish. Hist. Soc. 21:78-124.

_____. 1923. The Connecticut Irish in the Revolution: Numerous Celtic Names Listed in the Master Rolls. J. Amer. Irish Hist. Soc. 22:116-124.

_____. 1925. The Record of Sargent William Murphy. J. Amer. Irish Hist. Soc. 24:154-156.

_____. 1926. The Virginia Regiment. J. Amer. Irish Hist. Soc. 25:110-115.

_____. 1926. Washington's Irish Friends, J. Amer. Irish Hist. Soc. 25:344-369.

_____. 1927. Irish at the Front. Catholic World. 124:827-828.

_____. 1927. Members of Other Regiments Which Fought at Saratoga. J. Amer. Irish Hist. Soc. 26: 166-176.

_____. 1927. Morgans Riflemen at the Battle of Saratoga. J. Amer. Irish Hist. Soc. 26:154-165.

_____. 1928. An Interesting Example of the Extent of Irish Emigrations to the American Colonies. J. Amer. Irish Hist. Soc. 27:179-183.

_____. 1928. Proctor's Artillery in the Revolutionary War. J. Amer. Irish Hist. Soc. 27:176-178.

_____. 1928. The Commander-in-Chief's Guard. J. Amer. Irish Hist. Soc. 27:172-175.

_____. 1928. The Virginia Irish in the Revolution: An Answer to a Critic. J. Amer. Irish Hist. Soc. 27:237-253.

_____. 1930. The "Scotch Irish" in the War of the Revolution. J. Amer. Irish Hist. Soc. 28:47-54.

_____. 1937. George Washington's Associations with the Irish. Kennedy, New York.

_____. 1937. The Irish at Bunker Hill. Devin Adair, New York.

O'Connell, J. C. 1903. The Irish in the Revolution and the Civil War, Rev. and enlarg. embracing the Spanish American and Philippine Wars. Trades Unionist Press, Washington.

O'Connell, M. 1976. The American Revolution and Ireland. Eire. 11:3:3-12.

O'Flaherty, P. 1973. James Huston: A Forgotten Irish-American Patriot. Irish Sword. 11:43:39-47.

Onahan, W. J. 1910. The French-Irish Brigades in the War of Independence. J. Amer. Irish Hist. Soc. 9:416-420.

O'Sheil, K. R. 1920. The Irish in the American Revolution. In: K. R. Shiel, The Making of the Republic. Talbot Press, Dublin. pp. 126-139.

Petty, A. M. 1937. History of the 37th Regiment New York Volunteers. J. Amer. Irish Hist. Soc. 31:101-137.

Phelan, T. P. 1922. Thomas Fitzsimmons Patriot, Soldier and Statesman. J. Amer. Irish Hist. Soc. 21:157-164.

Power, W. 1969. The Enigma of the Patricios. Eire/Ireland. 4:4:7-12.

_____. 1975. Facets of the Mexican War. The Recorder. 36:135-143.

Purcell, R. J. 1922. Ireland and the America's Civil War. Catholic World. 115:72-84.

_____. 1932. James Shields: Soldier and Statesman. Studies: An Irish Quart. Rev. 21: 73-87.

Sheridan, F. 1927. Influence of the Irish People in the Formation of the United States. Ill. Cath. Hist. Rev. 9:377-381.

Smith, H. F. 1963. Mulligan and the Irish Brigade. J. Ill. St. Hist. Soc. 56:164-175.

Smith, S. S. 1975. The Search for Molly Pitcher. Daughters of the American Revolution Magz. 109: 4:292-295.

Stock, L. F. 1939. The Irish Parliament and the American Revolution. U.S. Cath. Hist. Soc. Rec. 30:11-29.

Sweeny, W. M. 1927. The Irish Soldier in the War with Mexico. J. Amer. Irish Hist. Soc. 26:255-259.

_____. 1928. Brigadier General Thomas W. Sweeney U.S. Army. J. Amer. Irish Hist. Soc. 27: 257-272.

Tangwall, W. F. 1962. Immigrants in the Civil War: Some American Reactions. Univ. of Chicago. Ph.D. dissertation.

Tanner, H. H. 1965. The Delaney Murder Case. Fla. Hist. Quart. 44:1/2:136-149.

VanDyke, M. A. 1976. Timothy Murphy: The Man and the Legend. New York Folklore. 2:1/2:87-110.

Woodruff, C. A. 1912. The Irish Soldier in the Civil War. J. Amer. Irish Hist. Soc. 11:154-159.

Chapter 7:   IRISH-AMERICA AND IRISH NATIONALISM

Adams, G. H.   1886.   Our State Department and Extradition. Amer. Law Rev. 20:540-552.

Akenson, D. A.   1973.   The United States and Ireland. Harvard Univ., Cambridge, Massachusetts.

Anon.   1871.   Fenianism By One Who Knows.   Contemporary Review.   19:301-316.

Bagenal, H.   1882.   The American Irish and the Influence on Irish Politics.   K. Paul, Trench, Co., London.   (Reprinted 1971 Ozer, New York).

Blake, N. M.   1935.   The United States and the Irish Revolution 1914-1922.   Clark Univ.   Ph.D. dissertation.

Brannigan, C. J.   1977.   The Luke Dillon Case and the Welland Canal Explosion of 1900:   Non-Events in the History of the Niagra Frontier Region.   Niagra Frontier.   24:2:36-44.

Bromage, M. C.   1951.   DeValera Mission to America. South Atlantic Quart. 50:499-513.

Brown, S. A. J.   1977.   The Irish Question in Anglo-American Relations, 1914-1922.   Bradford Univ. Ph.D. dissertation.

Brown, T. N.   1953.   Nationalism and the Irish Peasant.   1800-1848.   Rev. of Politics.   15:4:403-445.

_____.   1956.   The Origins and Character of Irish-American Nationalism.   Rev. of Politics.   18:3:327-358.

_____.   1966.   Irish-American Nationalism, 1870-1890.   J. B. Lippincott, New York.

Buckley, J. P.   1974.   The New York Irish:   Their View of American Foreign Policy 1914-1921.   New York Univ.   Ph.D. dissertation.

Calkin, H. L. 1954. The United States Government and the Irish. Irish Historical Studies, 9:28-52.

Carroll, F. M. 1978. American Opinion and the Irish Question 1910-1923. St. Martins Press, New York.

Cassidy, M. A. 1941. The History of the Fenian Movement in the United States, 1848-1866, and its Background in Ireland and America. Univ. of Buffalo. Masters thesis.

Colton, K. E. 1940. Parnell's Mission to Iowa. Annals of Iowa,: A Hist. Quart. 22:312-327.

Clark, D. I. 1970. Letters from the Underground: The Fenian Correspondence of James Gibbons. Rec. Amer. Cath. Hist. Soc., Philadelphia. 81:83-88.

_____. 1971. Militants of the 1860's: The Philadelphia Fenians. Penna. Magz. Hist. and Biog. 95:98-108.

_____. 1977. Irish Blood: Northern Ireland and the American Conscience. Kennikat Press, Port Washington, New York.

Cohalan, D. F. 1921. Our Economic Interest in Ireland. Forum. 65:59-67.

_____. 1921. Our Foreign Policy. Forum. 65: 187-196, 317-347.

Costigan, G. 1943. The Tragedy of Charles O'Conor: An Episode in Anglo-Irish Relations. American Historical Review. 49:1:32-54.

Creigton, R. J. 1882. Influence of Foreign Issues on American Politics. Internat. Rev. 13:182-190.

Cronin, S. 1972. The McGarrity Papers. Revelations of the Irish Revolutionary Movement in Ireland and America, 1900-1940. Anvil, Tralee, Kerry.

Cuddy, H. 1953. The Influence of the Fenian Movement on Anglo-American Relations, 1860-1872. St. Johns Univ. Ph.D. dissertation.

Cuddy, J. E. 1965. Irish-America and National Isolationism: 1914-1920. SUNY at Buffalo. Ph.D. dissertation. (reprinted, 1976, Arno).

_____. 1967. Irish-American Propagandists and American Neutrality, 1914-1917. Mid-America. 49: 4:252-74.

_____. 1969. Irish-Americans and the 1916 Elections: An Episode of Immigrant Adjustment. Amer. Quart. 21:228-243.

D'Arcy, W. 1947. The Fenian Movement in the United States, 1858-1886. Catholic Univ., Washington, D.C. (reprint, Russell and Russell, 1971).

Devoy, J. 1948. Devoy's Post Bag 1871-1928. (2 Vols.) C. J. Fallon, Dublin.

Donovan, H. D. A. 1930. Fenian Memories in Northern New York. J. Amer. Irish Hist. Soc. 28:148-152.

Duff, J. B. 1964. The Politics of Revenge: Ethnic Opposition to the Peace Policies of Woodrow Wilson. Columbia Univ. Ph.D. dissertation.

_____. 1968. The Versailles Treaty and the Irish Americans. J. Amer. Hist. 55:582-598.

Dwyer, T. R. 1977. American Efforts to Discredit de Valera During World War II. Eire-Ireland. 7:2: 20-33.

_____. 1977. Irish Neutrality and USA 1939-47. Rowman and Littlefield. Totowa, New Jersey.

Edwards, O. D. 1967. American Diplomats and Irish Coercion, 1880-83. J. Amer. Stud. 1:2:213-232.

Fitzpatrick, J. 1973. The Irish American and Sinn Fein. Triumph. 8:13-16.

99

Funchion, M. F. 1973. Chicago's Irish Nationalists, 1881-1890. Loyola Univ., Chicago. Ph.D. dissertation. (reprint, Arno, 1976).

_____. 1975. Irish Nationalists and Chicago's Politics in the 1880's. Eire. 10:2:3-18.

Gaffney, T. St. John. 1931. Breaking the Silence: England, Ireland, Wilson and the War. Liveright, New York.

Galbraith, J. S. 1947. United States and Ireland, 1916-1920. South Atlantic Quart. 46:192-203.

_____. 1949. United States, Britain and the Creation of the Irish Free State. South Atlantic Quart. 48:566-574.

Green, E. R. R. 1958. Fenians. History Today. 8:698-705.

Green, J. J. 1949. American Catholics and the Irish Land League, 1879-1922. Catholic Historical Rev. 35:19-42.

Griffin, G. W. H. and G. Christy. 1873. The Fenian Spy or John Bull in America. Happy Hours Co., New York.

Guptill, F. F. 1969. A Popular Bibliography of the Fenian Movement. Eire/Ireland. 4:2:18-25.

Hachey, T. E. 1975. British War Propaganda and American Catholics, 1918. Cath. Hist. Rev. 61:48-66.

Hazel, M. V. 1980. First Link: Parnell's American Tour, 1880. Eire-Ireland. 15:1:6-24.

Hendrick, B. J. 1925. The Life and Letters of Walter H. Page. Doubleday, Garden City, New York.

Hernon, J. M. 1966. The Irish Nationalists and the Southern Sucession. Civil War Hist. 4:43-53.

_____. 1968. Celts, Catholics and Copperheads: Ireland Views the American Civil War. Ohio State Univ. Press, Columbus.

Hernon, J. M., Jr. 1964. The Use of the American Civil War in the Debate Over Irish Home Rule. American Historical Review. 69:4:1022-1026.

Hoslett, S. D. 1940. The Fenian Brotherhood. Americana. 34:596-603.

Hunt, H. M. 1889. The Crime of the Century or the Assassination of Dr. Patrick Henry Cronin. Kochersperger, Chicago.

James, H. 1880. The Work of the Irish Leagues. Cassell, New York.

Jamison, A. 1942. Irish American the Irish Question and American Diploma, 1845-1921. Harvard Univ. Ph.D. dissertation.

Jeffrey-Jones, R. 1975. Massachusetts Labor and the League of Nation Controversy in 1919. Irish Hist. Studies. 19:76:396-416.

Jenkins, B. 1968. The British Government Sir John A. McDonald and the Fenian Claims. Can. Hist. Rev. 41:142-159.

_____. 1969. Fenians and Anglo-American Relations During Reconstruction. Cornell Univ., Ithaca.

Jones, W. D. 1967. Made in New York: A Plot to Kill the Queen. New York Hist. Soc. Quart. 51:311-325.

Kiernan, J. L. 1864. Ireland and America, Versus England, From a Fenian Point of View. G. W. Pattison, printer. Detroit.

King, C. L. 1909. The Fenian Movement. Univ. of Colorado Studies. 6:187-213.

Kraus, M. 1939. America and the Irish Revolutionary Movement in the Eighteenth Century. In the Era of the American Revolution. R. B. Morris, ed. Columbia Univ., New York.

Langan, M. 1937. General John O'Neill Soldier, Fenian and Leader of Irish Catholic Colonization in America. Univ. of Notre Dame. Masters thesis.

Laubenstein, W. J. 1960. The Emerald Whaler: A Saga of the Sea and Men Who Risked All for Freedom. Bobbs-Merrill. Indianapolis.

ᵧLeary, W. M. 1967. Woodrow Wilson, Irish-America and the Election, 1916. J. Amer. Hist. 54:57-72.

Leslie, S. 1917. The Irish Issue in its American Aspect. Charles Scribners, New York.

Mannion, L. F. (ed.) 1969. Constitution and By Laws of the Fenian Brotherhood of Colorado Territory. Eire/Ireland. 4:2:7-17.

Maxwell, K. R. 1967-68. Irish Americans and the Fight for Treaty Ratification. Public Opinion Quart. 31:620-641.

McCaffrey, L. J. 1973. Irish Nationalism and Irish Catholicism: A Study in Cultural Identity. Church History. 42:4:1-11.

_____. 1976. Irish Nationalism and the American Contribution. Arno Press, New York.

McCartan, P. 1932. With De Valera in America. Brentano, New York. Fitzpatrick Press, Dublin.

McDonnell, T. P. 1974. Catholic Press Reporting on Northern Ireland. Holy Cross Quart. 6:1-4:68-71.

McEnnis, J. T. 1889. The Clan-na Gael and the Murder of Dr. Patrick Henry Cronin. F. J. Schittze and J. W. Iliff. Chicago.

McGee, T. D. 1866. The Irish Position in Britain and in Republican North America. Longmoore, Montreal

McGinley, C. 1966. Irish-American's in Philadelphia and Their Involvement with the Irish Independence Movement. Temple Univ. Paper History Dept. Seminar.

McManamin, F. G. 1959. The American Years of John
Boyle O'Reilly, 1870-1890. Catholic Univ. Ph.D.
dissertation (reprinted, 1976, Arno).

McSweeney, E. F. 1919. Ireland is an American
Question. Friends of Irish Freedom, New York.

Minnick, W. C. 1953. Parnell in America. Speech
Monographs. 20:38-48.

Mitchell, A. 1967. The Fenian Movement in America.
Eire/Ireland. 2:6-10.

Moody, T. W. 1967. Irish-American Nationalism.
Irish Hist. Studies. 15:60:438-445.

Moriarty, T. F. 1980. The Irish-American Response to
Catholic Emancipation. The Cath. Hist. Rev., 66:3:353-373.

Morrow, R. L. 1934. The Negotiation for the Anglo-
American Treaty of 1870. Amer. Hist. Rev. 39:663-
681.

Murray, H. T. 1975. The Green and the Red Un-
blending: The Nat. Assn. for Irish Freedom, 1972-
1975. J. Ethnic Stud. 3:2:1-21.

Neidhardt, W. S. 1972. The American Government
and the Fenian Brotherhood: A study in mutual
political opportunism. Ontario Hist. 64:27-44.

_____. 1975. Fenianism in North America.
Penna. St. Univ. State College, Pennsylvania.

Noer, T. J. 1973. The American Government and the
Irish Question During World War I. South Atlantic
Quart. 72:1:95-114.

O'Broin, L. 1971. Fenian Fever: An Anglo-American
Dilemma. New York Univ., New York.

O'Connor, T. P. and R. McWade. 1886. Gladstone-
Parnell and the Great Irish Struggle. Robertson,
Toronto.

O'Doherty, K. 1957. Assignment America De Valera's Mission to the United States. DeTanko, New York.

O'Donnell, F. H. 1883. Fenianism Past and Present. Contemp. Rev. 43:747-766.

O'Donovan-Rossa, J. 1898. Rossa's Recollections 1858 to 1898. Mariners' Harbor, New York.

O'Grady, J. P. 1958. The Irish-American Influence in the Rejection of the Phelps-Roseberry Extradition Treaty of 1886. Univ. of Notre Dame. Masters thesis.

_____. 1963. Irish-Americans Woodrow Wilson and Self Determinations a Re-evaluation. Records of Am. Cath. Hist. Soc. of Philadelphia. 74:159-173.

_____. 1965. Irish-Americans and Anglo-America Relations, 1880-1888. Univ. of Pennsylvania. Ph.D. dissertation. (reprinted, 1976, Arno).

_____. 1967. The Irish. In: The Immigrants Influence on Wilson Peace Politics. J. P. O'Grady, ed. Univ. of Kentucky, Lexington. pp. 56-84.

_____. 1967. The Irish. In: The Immigrants Influence on Wilson's Foreign Policies. D. C. Heath, Jr. Lexington, Massachusetts. pp. 54-84.

O'Hara, M. M. 1919. Chief and Tribune: Parnell and Davitt. Maunsel, Dublin.

O'Reilly, J. B. 1882. Irelands Opportunity, Will it be Lost. Amer. Cath. Quart. Rev. 7:114-120.

_____. 1886. At Last. North Amer. Rev. 142:104-110.

Pease, Z. Q. and G. S. Anthony. 1897. The Catalpa Expedition. G. S. Anthony, New Bedford, Massachusetts.

Pieper, E. 1931. The Fenian Movement. Univ. of Illinois. Ph.D. dissertation.

Ryan, D. 1937. The Phoenix Flame: A Study of Fenianism and John Devoy. Barker, London.

_____. 1969. The Fenian Chief: A Biography of James Stephens. University of Miami Press, Coral Gables, Florida.

Sammon, P. J. 1951. The History of the Irish National Federation of America. Catholic Univ. Masters thesis.

Savage, J. 1968. Fenian Heroes and Martyrs. P. Donahoe, Boston.

Savory, D. L. 1959. The Irish Republic and Neutrality in 1941. Contemp. Rev. 196:1:164-166.

_____. 1959. The Irish Republic and Neutrality in 1941. Contemp. Rev. 196:2:221-224.

Schofield, W. G. 1956. Seek For a Hero - The Story of John Boyle O'Reilly. Kenedy, New York.

Self, E. 1883. The Abuse of Citizenship. North Amer. Rev. 136:541-556.

Shannon, W. V. 1975. Northern Ireland and America's Responsibility. The Recorder. 36:28-42.

Shore, L. 1917. The Irish Issue in Its American Aspect. Scribners, New York.

Short, K. R. M. 1979. The Dynamite War: Irish-American Bombers in Victorian Britain. Humanities Press, Atlantic Highlands, New Jersey.

Sowles, E. A. 1880. History of Fenianism and Fenian Raids in Vermont. Vermont Hist. Proceedings.

Splain, J. J. 1924. The Irish Movement in the United States Since 1911. In: The Voice of Ireland. John Heywood, Ltd., Dublin.

Strauss, E. 1951. Irish Nationalism and British Democracy. Methuen & Co., London. (Columbia Univ., New York).

Sullivan, A. 1884. The American Republic and the Irish National League of America. Amer. Cath. Quart. Rev. 9:35-44.

Sullivan, M. 1971. Fighting for Irish Freedom: St. Louis Irish-Americans, 1918-1922. Missouri Hist. Rev. 65:184-206.

_____. 1972. Constitutionalism Revolution and Culture, Irish-American Nationalism in St. Louis, 1902-1914. Mo. Hist. Soc. Bull. 28:4:234-245.

Tansill, C. C. 1957. America and the Fight for Irish Freedom, 1866-1922. Devin-Adair, New York.

Tarpey, M. V. 1969. The Role of Joesph McGarrity in the Struggle for Irish Independence. St. Johns Univ. Ph.D. dissertation. (reprint, Arno, 1976).

Wade, M. 1950. The French Parish and Survivance in 19th Century New England. Cath. Hist. Rev. 36:163-189.

Walker, M. G. 1969. The Fenian Movement. Ralph Myles, Colorado Springs, Colorado.

Walsh, J. P. 1962. DeValera in United States, 1919. Rec. Amer. Cath. Hist. Soc. Phila. 73:92-107.

_____. 1967. Woodrow Wilson Historians vs. the Irish. Eire/Ireland. 2:2:55-66.

Ward, A. J. 1968. America and the Irish Problem 1899-1921. Irish Historical Studies. 16:61:64-90.

_____. 1969. Ireland and Anglo-American Relations, 1899-1921. Univ. Toronto, Toronto.

Whalen, R. J. 1964. The Founding Father: The Story of Joseph P. Kennedy and the Family He Raised to Power. Signet Books, New York.

Whittemore, C. P. 1961. A General of the Revolution John Sullivan of New Hampshire. Columbia Univ., New York.

Winkler, I. 1936. The Fenian Movement and Anglo-
American Diplomacy in the Reconstruction Period.
New York Univ. Masters thesis.

Chapter 8:  IRISH-AMERICAN RELIGION   AND THE
             CATHOLIC CHURCH

Abell, A. I.  1946.  Monsignor Ryan: A Historical
Interpretation.  Rev. Politics. 8:128-134.

_____.  1960.  American Catholicism and Social
Action:  A Search for Social Justice, 1865-1950.
Hanover House, Garden City, New York.

Abramson, H. J.  1971.  Ethnic Diversity Within
Catholicism:  A Comparative Analysis of Contemporary
and Historical Religion.  J. Social History. 4:4:
359-388.

_____.  1973.  Ethnic Diversity in Catholic
America.  Wiley, New York.

_____.  1975.  The Religio-Ethnic Factor and the
American Experience. Ethnicity. 2:163-177.

Agonito, J.  1977.  The Papers of John Carroll.
Cath. Hist. Rev. 63:583-592.

Ahern, P. H.  1948.  The Catholic University of
America, 1887-1896.  The Rectorship of John L.
Keane.  Catholic Univ., Washington.

_____.  1955.  The Life of John J. Keane.  Bruce,
Milwaukee.

Betz, E. K.  1960.  Priest, Patriot and Leader:
The Story of Archbishop Carroll of Carrollton.
Harvard, Cambridge, Massachusetts.

Biever, B. F.  1965.  Religion, Culture and Values:
A Cross Cultural Analysis of Motivational Factors in
Native Irish and American Irish Catholicism.  Univ.
Penna.  Ph.D. dissertation. (report, Arno, 1976).

Bland, St. Joan.  1951.  Hiberian Crusade, The Story
of the Catholic Total Abstinence Union of America.
The Catholic University of America Press.  Washington, D.C.

Blanshard, P. 1953. The Irish and Catholic Power, an American Interpretation. Beacon, Boston.

Bowler, M. 1933. A History of Catholic Colleges for Women in the United States of America. Catholic University. Ph.D. dissertation.

Boyle, M. I. 1947. Early History of the Catholic Church in the Saginaw. Univ. of Notre Dame, Notre Dame, Indiana. Masters thesis.

Brann, H. A. 1892. Most Reverend John Hughes. Dodd and Mead, New York.

Brown, T. N. 1970. The United States of America: The Irish Layman. Gill and Macmillan, Dublin.

Browne, H. J. 1949. The Catholic Church and the Knights of Labor. Catholic Univ., Washington.

Buczek, D. S. 1976. Polish American Priests and the American Catholic Hierarchy: A View from the Twenties. Polish Amer. Stud. 33:1:34-43.

Buetow, H. A. 1970. The Singular Benefit: The Story of Catholic Education in the United States. Macmillan, New York.

Burton, K. K. 1954. Childrens Shepherd. Kenedy, New York.

Byrne, W., ed. 1899. History of the Catholic Church in the New England States. Boston.

Cadden, J. P. 1944. Historiography of the American Catholic Church, 1785-1943. Catholic Univ., Washington, D.C.

Campion, D. R. 1949. Survey of American Social Catholicism, 1930-1940. St. Louis University, Masters thesis.

Carey, P. 1975. John England and Irish-American Catholicism, 1815-1842: A Study of Conflict. Fordham Univ. Ph.D. dissertation.

_____. 1977. A National Church: Catholic Search for Identity: 1820-1829. Center for the Study of American Catholicism. Working Paper Series No. 3. Univ. Notre Dame.

_____. 1979. Voluntaryism: An Irish Catholic Tradition. Church History. 48:1:49-62.

Casper, H. W. 1966. History of the Church in Nebraska. VI. The Church on the Northern Plains 1838-1874. Bruce, Milwaukee.

_____. 1966. History of the Church in Nebraska. VII. The Church on the Fading Frontier 1864-1910. Bruce, Milwaukee.

_____. 1966. History of the Church in Nebraska. VIII. Catholic Chapter in Nebraska Immigration. Bruce, Milwaukee.

Cerny, K. H. 1955. Monsignor John A. Ryan and the Social Action Department. Yale Univ. Ph.D. dissertation.

Clancy, R. J. 1932. Francis Patrick Kenrick and the Oxford Movement in America. Univ. of Notre Dame. Masters thesis.

Clark, D. J. 1977. The Irish Catholics: A Postponed Perspective. In: Immigrants and Religion in Urban America. ed. R. M. Miller and T. D. Marzik. Temple Univ., Philadelphia. pp. 48-68.

Clarke, R. A. 1888. Lives of the Deceased Bishops of the Catholic Church in the United States. 3 Vols. Clarke, New York.

Cogley, J. 1973. Catholic America. Dial Press, New York.

_____. 1973. The Irish Invasion. In: Catholic America, by J. Cogley. Dial Press, New York. pp. 28-51.

111

_____. 1973. Varieties of Catholicism. In: Catholic America, P. Gleason, ed. Dial Press, New York. pp. 143-167.

_____. 1975. Varieties of Catholicism. In: Majority and Minority, N. Yetman and C. H. Steele eds. Allyn-Bacon, Boston. pp. 252-260.

Connors, E. M. 1951. Church-State Relationships in Education in the State of New York. Catholic Univ., Washington.

Constantius, Brother. 1911. The Christian Brothers in the United States. Cath. Educ. Rev. 1:313-323.

Crosby, D. F. 1978. God, Church and Flag: Senator Joseph McCarthy and the Catholic Church. Univ. North Carolina, Chapel Hill.

Cross, R. D. 1958. The Emergence of Liberal Catholicism in America. Harvard, Cambridge, Massachusetts.

_____. 1959. The Changing Image of Catholicism in America. Yale Univ. Rev. 48:562-575.

_____. 1965. Origins of the Catholic Parochial Schools in America. Amer. Benedictine Rev. 16:194-209.

Curley, M. J. 1916. The Aim of Catholic Education. Cath. Educ. Rev. 12:1:18-26.

Curran, E. R. 1974. Conservative Thought and Strategy in the School Controversy, 1891-1893. Notre Dame J. Education. 7:144-162.

_____. 1974. Michael Augustine Corrigan and the Shaping of Conservative Catholicism in America, 1878-1895. Yale Univ. Ph.D. dissertation.

Cutler, J. H. 1970. Cardinal Cushing of Boston. Hawthorn, New York.

Dabney, V. 1949. Dry Messiah: The Life of Bishop Canon. Knopf, New York.

Dever, J. 1965. Cushing of Boston: A Candid Portrait. Bruce, Humphries, Boston.

Diffley, J. E. 1959. Catholic Reaction to American Public Education, 1792-1852. Univ. of Notre Dame. Ph.D. dissertation.

Dohen, D. 1967. Nationalism and American Catholicism. Sheed and Ward, New York.

Dolan, J. 1975. The Immigrant Church: New York's Irish and German Catholics, 1815-1865. John Hopkins, Baltimore.

_____. 1978. Catholic Revivalism. The American Experience 1830-1900. University of Notre Dame. Notre Dame, Indiana.

Donohoe, J. M. 1953. The Irish Benevolent Union 1889-1893. Catholic Univ. Press, Washington.

Duclos, W. E. 1972. Crisis of an American Catholic Modernist: Toward the Moral Absolutism of William L. Sullivan. Church Hist. 41:3:369-384.

Dwyer, J. T. 1976. Condemned to the Mines: The Life of Eugene O'Connell 1815-1891: Pioneer Bishop of Northern California and Nevada. Vantage Press, New York.

Egan, P. K. 1969. The Influence of the Irish on the Catholic Church in America in the 19th Century. National University of Ireland, Dublin.

Ellis, J. T. 1952. Church and State in the United States: A Critical Appraisal. Cath. Hist. Rev. 38:285-316.

_____. 1952. The Life of James Cardinal Gibbons, Archbishop of Baltimore 1834-1921. Bruce, Milwaukee.

_____. 1956. American Catholics and Intellectual Life. The Heritage Foundation, Chicago.

_____. 1961. St. Patrick in America. Amer. Benedictine Rev. 12:415-429.

_____. 1969. American Catholicism. Univ. of Chicago, Chicago.

Erbacher, S. A. 1931. Catholic Higher Education for Men in the United States 1850-1866. Catholic University. Ph.D. dissertation.

Evans, J. B. 1931. Irish Priests in Early Florida. J. Amer. Irish Hist. Soc. 32:74-78.

Fell, M. L. 1941. The Foundations of Nativism in American Textbooks, 1783-1860. Catholic University, Washington.

Fenton, J. H. 1951. Salt of the Earth: An Informal Portrait of Richard Cardinal Cushing. Coward-McCann, New York.

Finn, B. A. 1948. Twenty-Four American Cardinals. Humphries, Boston.

Flynn, A. 1962. The School Controversy in New York, 1840-1842 and its Effect on the Formation of Catholic Elementary School Policy. Univ. of Notre Dame. Ph.D. dissertation.

Folk, P. J. 1920. The Beginnings of Irish Catholic Journalism in America. Cath. Hist. Rev. 5:377-381.

Forster, W. P. 1965. Michael J. O'Shaughnessy and His Reform Program: A Catholic Businessman's Interpretation of the Papal Design for a New Social Order. Univ. of Notre Dame. Master thesis.

Fuchs, L. H. 1967. John Kennedy and American Catholicism. Meredith, New York.

Gaffey, J. P. 1965. The Life of Patrick William Riordan: Second Archbishop of San Francisco, 1841-1914. Catholic Univ. Ph.D. dissertation.

_____. 1973. The Changing of the Guard: The
Rise of Cardinal O'Connell of Boston. Cath. Hist.
Rev. 59:2:225-244.

Garraghan, G. J. 1921. The Catholic Church in
Chicago, 1673-1871. Chicago.

Gibbons, J. C. 1916. A Retrospect of Fifty Years.
2 Vols. Murphy, Baltimore.

Gleason, P. 1976. The Main Street Anchors. John
Carroll and Catholic Higher Education. Rev. Politics.
38:576-613.

_____. ed. 1970. Catholicism in America.
Harper & Row, New York.

Greeley, A. M. 1967. The Catholic Experience.
Doubleday, Garden City, New York.

_____. 1977. The American Catholic: A Self
Portrait. Basic Books, New York.

Griffen, C. S. 1961. Converting the Catholics:
American Benevolent Societies and the Ante-Bellum
Crusade Against the Church. Cath. Hist. Rev.
47:325-341.

Grozier, R. J. 1966. The Life and Times of John
Carroll, Archbishop of Baltimore. Encyclopedia,
New York.

Hackett, J. D. 1936. Bishops of the United States
of Irish Birth or Descent. Amer. Irish Hist. Soc.,
New York.

Haggerson, M. E. 1942. The History of the Diocese
of Mobile from 1826 to 1859. Univ. of Notre Dame.
Masters thesis.

Hassard, J. R. G. 1866. Life of the Most Reverend
John Hughes: First Archbishop of New York. Apple-
ton, New York.

Haughey, M. C. J. 1953. A Candle Lighted. Amer.
Cath. Hist. Soc. Rev. 64:113-120.

Hayes, F. H. 1965. Michigan Catholicism in the Era of the Civil War. Centennial Observance Commission, Lansing.

Heming, H. H. 1895. The Catholic Church in Wisconsin. Catholic Historical Publ. Co., Milwaukee.

Hennessey, J. 1970. The Distinctive Tradition of American Catholicism. In: Catholicism in America. P. Gleason, ed. Harper and Row, 28-44.

_____. 1978. An 18th Century Bishop: John Carroll of Baltimore. Archivium Historiae Pontificiae. 16:171-204.

Holmes, J. D. 1967. Irish Priests in Spanish Natchez. J. Miss. Hist. 29:169-180.

Hueston, R. F. 1972. The Catholic Press and Nativism, 1840-1860. Univ. of Notre Dame. Ph.D. dissertation. (reprinted, 1976, Arno).

Hughes, J. 1866. Complete Works of the Most Reverend John Hughes. Kehoe, New York (L. Kehoe ed.).

Ireland, John. 1897. The Church and Modern Society. D. H. McBride and Co., Chicago.

Irick, M. A. 1939. Early Catholicity in the Sandusky Region Prior to 1847. Univ. of Notre Dame. Masters thesis.

Ives, J. M. 1935. The Catholic Contribution to Religious Liberty in Colonial America. Cath. Hist. Rev. 21:283-298.

Kane, J. J. 1953. Catholic Separatism. Commonwealth. 58:293-296.

_____. 1955. Catholic Protestant Conflicts in America. Regnery, Chicago.

Kelly, M. G. 1940. Irish-Catholic Colonies and Colonization Projects in the United States, 1795-1860. Studies: An Irish Quart. Rev. 29:95-110, 447-465.

Kinzer, D. L. 1964. An Episode of Anti-Catholicism: The American Protective Association. Univ. Washington, Seattle.

Kunkle, N. M. 1974. Bishop Bernard J. McQuaid and Catholic Education. Univ. of Notre Dame. Ph.D. dissertation.

_____. 1976. Christian Free School's Bishop Bernard McQuaid's 19th Century Plan. Notre Dame J. Education. 7:1:18-27.

Lally, F. J. 1962. The Catholic Church in a Changing America. Little, Brown, Boston.

Lannie, V. P. 1968. Public Money and Parochial Education: Bishop Hughes, Governor Seward and the New York School Controversy. Case Western Reserve University, Cleveland.

_____. 1970. Catholics, Protestants and Public Education. In: Catholicism in America. P. Gleason, ed. Harper and Row, New York. pp. 45-57.

Larkin, E. 1976. The Historical Dimensions of Irish Catholicism. Arno Press, New York.

Leslie, S. 1917. Celt: The Saxon and the New Scene. Dublin Rev. 160:286-292.

_____. 1918. German and Irish Element in the American Melting Pot. Dublin Rev. 163:258-283.

Linehan, J. C. and T. H. Murray. 1898. Irish Schoolmasters in the American Colonies, 1640-1775. Amer. Irish Hist. Soc., Washington.

Linkh, R. M. 1975. American Catholicism and European Immigrants (1900-1924). Center for Migration Studies, Staten Island, New York.

Lord, R. H. et al. 1944. History of the Archdiocese
of Boston. Sheed and Ward, New York.

Luebke, F. C. 1976. Church History from the Bottom
Up. Rev. Amer. Hist. 4:1:68-72.

Manion, M. C. 1953. Principles of Catechetic
Instruction According to Reverend Peter C. Yorke.
Dominican College. Masters thesis.

Maynard, T. 1960. The Story of American Catholicism
2 Vols. Doubleday, New York.

McAllister, L. G. 1954. Thomas Campbell (1763-1854)
Man of the Book. Bethany, St. Louis, Missouri.

McAvoy, T. T. 1948. The Formation of the Catholic
Minority in the U.S. 1820-1860. Rev. of Politics.
10:13-24.

_____. 1950. Bishop John Lancaster and the
Catholic Minority. Review of Politics. 12:1:3-19.

_____. 1952. The Catholic Minority in the Uni-
ted States, 1789-1821. U.S. Cath. Hist. Soc. Rec.
Stud. 39-40:33-50.

_____. 1954. Orestes Brownson and American
History. Cath. Hist. Rev. 40:257-268.

_____. 1960. Roman Catholicism and the American
Way of Life. Univ. of Notre Dame, Notre Dame,
Indiana.

_____. 1964. Irish Clergyman in the United
States. Records Amer. Cath. Hist. Soc., Philadelphia. 75:6-38.

_____. 1966. Public Schools vs. Catholic Schools
and James McMaster. Rev. Politics. 28:1:19-46.

_____. 1967. Father O'Hara of Notre Dame: The
Cardinal Archbishop of Philadelphia. Univ. of Notre
Dame, Notre Dame, Indiana.

_____. 1969. History of the Catholic Church in the United States. Univ. of Notre Dame, Notre Dame, Indiana.

_____. 1970. The United States of America: The Irish Clergyman. Gill and Macmillan, Dublin.

McAvoy, T. T. and T. N. Brown. 1970. History of Irish Catholicism, Vol. 6, Fas. 2, The U.S.A. Gill and Macmillan, Dublin.

McCadden, J. J. 1964. Bishop Hughes versus the Public School Society of New York. Cath. Hist. Rev. 50:188-207.

_____. 1966. New York's School Crisis of 1840-1842: Its Irish Antecedants. Thought. 41:561-588.

McCaffrey, L. J. 1974. Catholicism and Irish Identity. Holy Cross Quart. 6:1-4:72-80.

McCullough, A. M. 1895. The Experience of Seventy Years. Tribune Job Press, Minneapolis.

McDonald, R. R. 1966. Father Charles Owen Rice: The Study of a Catholic Radical. Univ. of Notre Dame. Masters thesis.

McDonnell, T. P. 1974. Catholic Press Reporting on Northern Ireland. Holy Cross Quart. 6:1-4:68-71.

McElroy, R. M. 1914. Address. J. Amer. Irish Hist. Soc. 13:72-80.

McEniry, B. M. 1953. Women of Decision: The Life of Mother Mary Xavier Mehegan (1825-1915): Foundress of the Sisters of Charity of Saint Elizabeth Convent, New Jersey. Macmillan, New York.

McKeown, H. C. 1886. The Life and Labors of Most Reverend John Joseph Lynch, First Archbishop of Toronto. J. A. Sadlier. Montreal and Toronto.

McNamara, R. F. 1944. Trusteeism in the Atlantic States 1785-1863. Cath. Hist. Rev. 30:135-154.

119

Meagher, W. J. and W. J. Grattan. 1966. The Spires
of Fenwick: The History of the College of Holy
Cross, 1843-1863. Vantage, New York.

Melville, A. M. 1955. John Carroll of Baltimore,
Founder of the American Catholic Hierarchy. Scribner's. New York.

Meyers, M. A. 1964. The Childrens Crusade: Philadelphia Catholics and the Public Schools, 1840-1844.
Rec. Amer. Cath. Hist. Soc., Philadelphia. 75:103-
127.

Moran, D. M. 1950. Anti-Catholicism in Early
Marland Politics: The Protestant Revolution. Rec.
Amer. Cath. Hist. Soc., Philadelphia. 61:213-236.

_____. 1950. Anti-Catholicism in Early Maryland
Politics: The Puritan Influence. Rec. Amer. Cath.
Hist. Soc., Philadelphia. 61:139-154.

Moriarity, T. F. 1958. Agitation in the United
in Behalf of Catholic Emanicipation as Seen Through
The Truth Teller, 1825-1830. Univ. of Notre Dame.
Masters thesis.

Morrissey, T. H. 1976. A Controversial Reformer.
Archbishop John Ireland and His Educational Belief.
Notre Dame J. Educ. 77:1:63-75.

_____. 1975. Archbishop John Ireland and the
Faribault-Stillwater School Plan of the 1890's: A
Reappraisal. Univ. of Notre Dame. Ph.D. dissertatio

Moynihan, J. H. 1933. Archbishop Ireland. Acta et
Dicta. 6:12-35.

_____. 1953. The Life of Archbishop John Ire-
land. Harper, New York.

Nolan, H. J. 1948. The Most Reverend Francis Pat-
rich Kenrick: Third Bishop of Philadelphia, 1830.
Amer. Cath. Hist. Soc., Philadelphia, Pennsylvania.

O'Brien, D. J. 1966. American Catholicism and the Diaspora. Cross-Currents. 16:307-324.

_____. 1968. American Catholics and Social Reform. The New Deal Years. Oxford, New York.

O'Brien, M. J. 1912. Some Early Irish Settlers and Schoolmasters in New Jersey. J. Amer. Irish Hist. Soc. 11:121-130.

_____. 1917. Early Irish Schoolmasters in New England. Cath. Hist. Rev. 3:52-71.

_____. 1919. Irish Pioneers and Schoolmasters in Butler County, Pennsylvania. J. Amer. Irish Hist. Soc. 18:198-204.

_____. 1926. Irish Schoolmasters in the American Colonies. J. Amer. Irish Hist. Soc. 25:35-61.

_____. 1926. Some Irish Schoolmasters of Old New York and a Few Irish Schoolmasters of Its Early Days. Recorder. 3:7:6-8.

_____. 1928. Irish Schoolmasters in the City of New York. J. Amer. Irish Hist. Soc. 27:141-165.

O'Brien, T. D. 1933. Dillon O'Brien. Acta et Dicta. 5:67-77.

O'Connell, J. J. 1879. Catholicity in the Carolinas and Georgia, 1820-1857. Sadlier, New York.

O'Connell, W. 1934. Recollections of Seventy Years. Houghton-Mifflin, Boston.

O'Daniel, V. F. 1920. The Rev. Edward Dominic Fenwick. Pustet, New York.

O'Dea, T. F. 1956. The Catholic Immigrant and the American Scene. Thought. 31:251-270.

O'Donnell, J. H. 1939. The Catholic Church in Northern Indiana, 1830-1857. Cath. Hist. Rev. 25:135-145.

O'Dwyer, G. F. 1921. Ann Glover First Martyr to the Faith in New England. U.S. Cath. Hist. Soc. Rec. and Stud. 15:70-78.

O'degard, P. H. 1960. Catholicism and Elections in the United States. In: Religion and Politics, P. H. Odegard ed. Rutgers, New Brunswick, New Jersey.

O'Fahey, C. J. 1975. Reflections on the St. Patricks Day Orations of John Ireland. Ethnicity. 2:3:244-251.

O'Gorman, T. 1895. A History of the Roman Catholic Church in the United States. New York.

O'Grady, J. 1930. Catholic Charities in the United States History and Problems. Catholic Univ., Washington.

O'Hara, E. V. and R. J. Purcell. 1948. Archbishop Ireland: Two Appreciations. College of St. Thomas, Minneapolis.

O'Hearn, D. J. 1898. Fifty Years at St. Johns Cathedral 1847-1897. St. Johns Central, Milwaukee.

O'Mahony, T. 1972. The Irish Churches and the Credibility Gap. America. 127:440-442.

O'Meara, J. B. 1911. The Mission of the Irish Race in the United States. J. Amer. Irish Hist. Soc. 10:105-113.

O'Reilly, B. 1890. John McHale, His Life, Times and Correspondence. 2 vols. F. Pustet and Company, New York and Cincinnati.

Onahan, W. J. 1917. A Chapter of Catholic Colonization. Acta et Dicta. 5:1:67-77.

Overmoehle, M. H. 1941. The Anti-Clerical Activities of the Forty-Eighters in Wisconsin, 1848-1860. St. Louis Univ. Ph.D. dissertation.

Pare, B. 1951. The Catholic Church in Detroit 1701-1888. Gabriel Richard Press, Detroit.

Phelan, T. P. 1935. Catholics in Colonial Days. Gale Research, Detroit (reprint, 1977).

Pratt, J. W. 1965. Religious Conflict in the Development of the New York City Public School System. History of Educ. Quart. 5:110-120.

Purcell, R. J. 1934. Education and Irish School-masters in Maryland National Period. Cath. Educ. Rev. 32:198-207.

_____. 1934. Education and Irish Teachers in Colonial Maryland. Cath. Educ. Rev. 32:143-153.

_____. 1934. Schools and Early Irish Teachers in New Hampshire. Cath. Educ. Rev. 32:608-618.

_____. 1934. Some Early Teachers in Connecticut. Cath. Educ. Rev. 32:332-338.

_____. 1935. Education and Irish Schoolmasters in Colonial Massachusetts. Cath. Educ. Rev. 33: 467-479.

_____. 1935. Vermont: Schools and Early Irish Teachers. Cath. Educ. Rev. 33:277-281.

_____. 1936. Education and Irish Teachers in Early Kentucky. Cath. Educ. Rev. 34:360-369.

_____. 1936. Education and Irish Teachers in Massachusetts 1789-1865. Cath. Educ. Rev. 34:87-96, 159-166.

_____. 1936. Pioneer Irish Educators in Tennessee. Cath. Educ. Rev. 34:406-413.

_____. 1936. Rhode Islands Early Schools and Irish Teachers. Cath. Educ. Rev. 34:402-415.

_____. 1940. Irish Educational Contribution to Pennsylvania in the National Period. Cath. Educ. Rev. 38:467-80, 537-549.

_____. 1946. John A. Ryan: Prophet of Social Justice. Studies An Irish Quart. Review. 35:153-174.

Quinlan, R. J. 1937. Browth and Development of Catholic Education in the Archdiocese of Boston. Cath. Hist. Rev. 22:27-41.

Reynolds, F. L. 1921. The Ancient Order of Hibernians. Ill. Cath. Hist. Rev. 4:22-33.

Riley, A. J. 1936. Catholicism in New England to 1788. Catholic Univ., Washington.

Roohan, J. E. 1952. American Catholics and the Social Question, 1865-1900. Yale Univ. Ph.D. dissertation. (report, Arno, 1976).

Rosenberg, C. 1971. Religion and the Rise of the American City: The New York City Mission Movement, 1812-1870. Cornell Univ. Ithaca, New York.

Rousseau, R. 1969. Bishop John England and American - Church State Theory. St. Paul Univ. Ph.D. dissertation.

Russo, N. J. 1969. Three Generations of Italians in New York City: Their Religious Acculturation. Int. Mig. Rev. 3:2:3-17.

Sanders, J. W. 1977. 19th Century Boston Catholics and the School Question. Center for the Study of American Catholicism. Working Paper Series No. 2. Univ. of Notre Dame.

_____. 1977. The Education of an Urban Minority: Catholics in Chicago, 1833-1965. Oxford Univ., New York.

Sandman, E. A. 1943. James Alphonsus McMaster and the Controversy over Papal Infallibility. Univ. of Notre Dame. Masters thesis.

Sharp, J. K. 1954. History of the Diocese of Brooklyn, 1853-1953. 20 Vols. Fordham Univ., New York.

Shaughnessy, G. 1925. Has the Immigrant Kept the Faith? A Study of Immigration and Catholic Growth in the United States, 1790-1920. Macmillan, New York.

Shea, J. G. 1892. History of the Catholic Church in the United States, 4 Vols. New York.

Sheppard, J. H. 1910. The Irish in Protestant Denominations in America. J. Amer. Irish Hist. Soc. 9:93-109.

_____. 1925. Irish Preachers and Educators in the Early History of the Presbyterian Church in America. J. Amer. Irish Hist. Soc. 24:162-174.

Smith, A. E. and V. Fitzpatrick. 1921. Cardinal Gibbons: Churchman and Citizen. O'Donovan, Baltimore.

Spalding, J. L. 1880. The Religious Mission of the Irish People and Catholic Colonization. The Catholic Publication Society Co., New York.

Stout, H. S. 1975. Ethnicity: The Vital Center of Religion in America. Ethnicity. 2:204-224.

Taylor, M. C. 1976. A History of the Foundations of Catholicism in Northern New York. U.S. Catholic Hist. Soc., New York (Monog. Series, 32).

Tehan, A. B. and J. Tehan. 1962. Prince of Democracy. James Cardinal Gibbons. Doubleday, New York.

Tourscher, F. E. 1930. The Hogan Schism and Trustee Troubles in St. Marys Church Philadelphia: 1820-1829. P. Reilly, Philadelphia.

Trisco, R. F. 1962. The Holy See and the Nascent Church in the Middle Western United States, 1826-1850. Georgian University Press, Rome, Georgia.

_____. ed. 1976. Catholic in America 1776-1976. Nat. Conf. Cath. Bishops, Comm. for Bicent, Washington, D. C.

Van Deusen, G. G. 1965. Seward and the School Question Reconsidered. J. Amer. Hist. 52:1:313-319.

Walsh, H. L. 1946. Hallowed Were the Gold Dust Trails. Univ. Santa Clara, Santa Clara, California.

Wangler, T. E. 1971. John Ireland and the Origins of Liberal Catholicism in the United States. Cath. Hist. Rev. 56:617-629.

Warkov, S. and A. M. Greeley. 1966. Parochial School Origins and Educational Achievement. Amer. Soc. Rev. 31:406-414.

Wayman, D. G. 1955. Cardinal O'Connell of Boston: A Biography of William Henry O'Connell, 1859-1944. Farrar, Straus, New York.

Weber, F. J. 1965. Catholicism in Colonial America. Homitetic and Pastoral Rev. 65:842-851.

_____. 1966. John Tracy Ellis, Historian of American Catholicism. The American Benedictine Review. 17:467-478.

_____. 1976. Americas Catholic Heritage: Some Bicentennial Reflections, 1776-1976. St. Paul's Editions, Boston.

Weisz, H. R. 1968. Irish-American and Italian-American Educational Views and Activities, 1870-1900: A Comparison. Columbia Univ. Ph.D. dissertation.

_____. 1972. Irish-American Attitudes and the Americanization of the English Language Parochial School. New York Hist. 53:157-176.

Westcroft, T. 1884-1886. A Memoir of the Very Rev. Michael Hurley, D. C., OSA. Rec. Amer. Cath. Hist. Soc., Philadelphia, 1:165-212.

Will, A. S. 1922. Life of Cardinal Gibbons, Archbishop of Baltimore. Dillon, New York.

Willis, G. 1972. Bare Ruined Choirs. Doubleday, Garden City, New York.

Winter, M. M. 1930. The Beginning of Catholicity in Minnesota. Univ. of Notre Dame. Masters thesis.

Woodbury, K. A. 1967. An Incident Between the French-Canadians and the Irish in the Diocese of Maine, 1906. New England Quart. 40:260-268.

Zwierlein, F. J. 1916. Catholic Beginnings in the Diocese of Rochester. Cath. Hist. Rev. 1:282-298.

_____. 1925-1927. The Life and Letters of Bishop McQuaid. 3 Vols. Art Print Shop, Rochester, New York.

_____. 1946. Letters of Archbishop Corrigan in Bishop McQuaid and Allied Documents. Art Print Shop, Rochester, New York.

Chapter 9:  THE SCOTCH-IRISH - MYTH OR REALITY

Anon.  1922.  Early Irish Settlers in Maine and New
Hampshire.  Sprague's J. Maine Hist. 10:29-31.

Barna, F.  1971.  The Frontiersman as Ethnic:  A
Brief History of the Scotch-Irish.  In:  Ethnic
Groups in the City.  O. Feinstein ed.  D.C. Heath,
Boston.  pp. 155-164.

Beckett, J. C.  1948.  Protestant Dissent in Ireland
1687-1780.  Faber and Faber, London.

Bolton, C. K.  1910.  Scotch-Irish Pioneers in
Ulster and America.  Bacon and Brown, Boston.

Bradley, A. G.  1912.  Ulster Scot in the United
States.  19th Century.  71:1121-33.

Chalkley, L.  1912.  Chronicles of the Scotch-Irish
Settlement in Virginia.  3 Vols.  Genealogical
Publ., Baltimore (reprinted, 1980).

Coolidge, R. D.  1910.  Scotch-Irish in New England.
New England Magz. N.S.  42:747-750.

Coyle, J. G.  1913.  The Scot, The Ulster Scot and
the Irish.  J. Amer. Irish. Hist.  Society. 12:103-
111.

Cummings, H. M.  1964.  Scots Breed and Susquehana.
Univ. of Pittsburgh, Pittsburgh.

Dickie, A. A.  1948.  Scotch-Irish Presbyterian
Settlers in Southern Wisconsin.  Wisc. Magz. Hist.
31:291-302.

Dickson, R. J.  1966.  Ulster Emigration to Colonial
America.  1718-1775.  Routledge-Kegan Paul, London.

Dinsmore, J. W.  1906.  The Scotch-Irish in America.
Winona Publ. Co., Chicago.

Dunaway, W. F.  1944.  Scotch-Irish of Colonial
Pennsylvania.  Shoe Strong Press, Archon, Connecticut.

Evans, E. E. 1949. Old Ireland and New England. Ulster J. Arch. 12:104-112.

_____. 1959. A Pennsylvanian Folk Festival. Ulster Folklife. 5:14-19.

_____. 1965. The Scotch-Irish in the New World: An Atlantic Heritage. J. Roy. Soc. of Antiquaries of Ireland. 95:39-49.

_____. 1969. The Scotch-Irish: Their Cultural Adaptation and Heritage in the American Old West. In: Essays in Scotch Irish History ERR Green ed. Routledge and Kegan Paul, London.

Farson, W. V. 1924. Henry McCullough and His Irish Settlement. North Carolina Booklet. 22:32-39.

Fisk, W. L. 1948. The Scotch-Irish in Central Ohio. Ohio Arch. Quart. 25:518-530.

Ford, H. J. 1915. The Scotch-Irish in America. Princeton Univ. Press, Princeton.

Garland, R. 1923. The Scotch-Irish in Western Pennsylvania. Western Penna. Historical Magz. 6:2: 65-105.

Glasgow, M. 1936. The Scotch Irish in Northern Ireland and the American Colonies. G. P. Putnam, New York.

Green, E. R. 1952. Scotch-Irish Emigration, an Imperial Problem. West Penna. Hist. Magz. 35:4:193-209.

Green, E. R. R. 1955. The Scotch-Irish and the Coming of the Revolution in North Carolina. Irish Hist. Stud. 7:77-86.

_____. ed. 1955. The Strange Humors that Drove the Scotch-Irish to America, 1729. William and Mary Quart. 12:113-123.

_____. 1960. Queenborough Township: Scotch-Irish Emigration and the Expansion of Georgia, 1763-1776. William and Mary Quart. 17:183-199.

_____. 1969. Essays in Scotch-Irish History. Routledge and Kegan Paul, London.

Green, S. S. 1915. Scotch-Irish in America. Hamilton, Worcester, Massachusetts.

Hanna, C. A. 1902. The Scotch-Irish. 2 Vol., G. P. Putnam's Sons, New York and London.

Hiner, M. 1933. The Scotch-Irish and Academies in the Transallegheny Frontier. Univ. West Virginia. Masters thesis.

Ireland, O. S. 1973. The Ethnic-Religious Dimension of Pennsylvania Politics 1778-1779. William and Mary Quart. 30:423-448.

Johnson, J. F. 1966. Scots and Scotch-Irish in America. Lerner, New York.

Kephart, H. 1921. Our Southern Highlanders. MacMillan, New York.

Kernohan, J. W. 1920. Ulster Pilgrim Fathers: An Irish Mayflower. Landmark. 2:691-694.

Klett, G. S. 1937. Presbyterianism in Colonial Pennsylvania. Univ. Pennsylvania, Philadelphia.

_____. 1953. Scotch-Irish Pioneering Along the Susquehanna River, Pennsylvania Hist. 20:165-179.

Latimer, W. T. 1902. Ulster Emigration to America. J. Roy Soc. Antiquaries of Ireland. 32:388-392.

Leach, D. E. 1966. The Northern Colonial Frontier 1607-1763. Holt-Rinehart-Winston, New York.

Lehman, W. C. 1978. Scottish and Scotch-Irish Contribution to Early American Life and Culture. Kennikat Press, Port Washington, New York.

Lemon, J. T. 1972. The Best Poor Man's Country: A Geographical Study of Early Southeastern Pennsylvania. Johns Hopkins, Baltimore.

Leyburn, J. G. 1962. The Scotch-Irish. Univ. of North Carolina, Chapel Hill.

_____. 1970. The Melting Pot: The Ethnic Group that Blended the Scotch-Irish. Amer. Herit. 22:28-31, 97-101.

Linehan, J. C. 1888. The Irish-Scots and the Scotch Irish. Granite Monthly. 11:17-31, 50-57, 85-95.

Lodge, H. C. 1891. The Distribution of Ability in the United States. Century Magz. 42:687-694.

MacCracken, H. M. 1912. The Scotch-Irish in America and in New York. New York State Hist. Assoc. Proc. 11:104-122.

MacLeod, W. C. 1967. Celts and Indians. In: Beyond the Frontier. P. Bohannon, ed. Natural History Press, Garden City, New York. pp. 23-41.

McCourt, D. 1964. County Derry and New England. County Londondery Handbook, N.D. :87-101.

Moffatt, J. 1934. Scotch-Irish of the Up-Country. So. Atlantic Quart. 33:137-151.

Moody, T. W. 1945. The Ulster Scots in Colonial and Revolutionary America. Studies. 34:52-69.

_____. 1946. Irish and Scotch-Irish in 18th Century America. Studies. 35:123-140.

Myers, A. C. 1902. Immigration of the Irish Quakers into Pennsylvania 1692-1750. Swarthmore, Pennsylvania (report 1964, Genealogical Publ., Baltimore).

O'Brien, M. J. 1915. Some Examples of the "Scotch-Irish" in America. J. Amer. Irish Hist. Soc. 14: 269-279.

_____. 1919. How the Descendants of Irish Settlers in America Were Written into History as Anglo-Saxons and Scotch Irish. J. Amer. Irish Hist. Soc. 18:99-109.

_____. 1923. Shipping Statistics of the Philadelphia Arstom House, 1733-1774 Refute the Scotch-Irish Theory. J. Amer. Irish Hist. Soc. 22:132-141.

O'Brien, M. J. 1925. The "Scotch-Irish" Myth. J. Amer. Irish Hist. Soc. 24:142-153.

_____. 1927. Irish in the Surrogate's Records Ulster County, New York. J. Amer. Irish Hist. Soc. 26:129-136.

_____. 1930. An Alleged First Census of the American People: A Criticism of William H. Clemen's Book. American Marriage Records Before 1699. Amer. Irish Hist. Soc., New York.

O'Connell, J. D. 1897. The Scotch-Irish Delusions in America. Washington, D.C.

Perry, A. L. 1891. Scotch-Irish in New England. Boston.

Phillips, J. D. 1950. George Duncan: Emigrant to Londonderry, New Hampshire and Founder of the Duncan Families of New England. Essex. Instit. Hist. Col. 86:247-256.

Pillsbury, H. 1922. Scotch-Irish and the History of Londonderry. Americana. 21:548-557.

Roche, J. J. 1899. The Scotch-Irish and Anglo-Saxon Fallacies. J. Amer. Irish Hist. Soc. 2:89-92.

Rowe, G. S. 1972. Thomas McKeen and the Coming of the Revolution. Penna. Magz. Hist. and Brog. 96:3-47.

Shepardson, F. W. 1902. Scotch and Irish in America. Dial. 33:325-326.

Smith, J. 1895. The Scotch-Irish, An Inquiry into the New and Mysterious Race that Sprang from a Hyphen. Illustrated American. 18:354-360.

_____. 1898. The Scotch-Irish Shibboleth Analyzed and Rejected. Amer. Irish Hist. Soc., Washington, D.C.

Stone, F. D. 1890. First Congress of Scotch-Irish in America. Penna. Magz. Hist. Biog. 14:68-71.

Wallace, E. M. 1925. Early Farmers in Exeter. Wis. Magz. Hist. 8:415-422.

Weatherford, W. D. 1955. Pioneers of Destiny: The Romance of the Appalachin People. Vulcan Press, Birmingham, Alabama.

Welch, R. F. 1979. The Scotch-Irish. Early American Life. 10:4:32-34, 66, 68.

Williams, E. M. 1923. The Scotch-Irish in Pennsylvania. Americana. 17:374-387.

Willis, W. 1859. Scotch-Irish Immigration to Maine and Presbyterianism in New England. Collections Maine Hist. Soc. 1st Series, 6:1-37.

Wilson, A. E. 1920. Paddy Wilson's Meeting House in Providence Plantations, 1791-1839. Pilgrim Press, Boston.

Wittke, C. 1967. The Colonial Emigration from Ireland. The Irish and Scotch Irish. Chapter 5. In: C. Wittke. We Who Built America. Case Western Reserve, Cleveland. pp. 44-66.

Chapter 10:  THE IRISH IN CANADA

Anon.  1953.  Franklin and the Fenian Battle of
Richards Farm.  Vermont Hist. Soc. News and Notes.
4:41-43.

Armstrong, C.  1929.  A Typical Example of Immigration into Upper Canada in 1819.  Ontario Historical Society Papers and Records. 25:5-11.

Ascher, E.  1915.  Number One Company Niagra.
Niagra Hist. Soc. 27:60-73.

Baker, W. M.  1977.  Timothy Warren Anglin 1822-
1896:  Irish Catholic Canadian, Univ. of Toronto,
Toronto.

Baldwin, D. O.  1973.  Political and Social Behavior in Ontario 1879-1891:  A Quantitative
Approach.  York Univ. Ph.D. dissertation.

Baldwin, P.  1969.  The Political Power of Thomas
Talbot.  Ontario Hist. 61:9-19.

Banks, M.  1957.  Edward Blacke, Irish Nationalist:
A Canadian Statesman in Irish Politics.  Univ. of
Toronto, Toronto.

Bleasdale, R. C.  1975.  Irish Labourers on the
Cornwall, Welland, and Williamsburg Canals in the
1840's.  Univ. Western Ontario.  Masters thesis.

Blegen, T. C.  1917-18.  A Plan for the Union of
British North America and the United States 1866.
Miss. Valley Hist. Rev. 4:470-83.

Boyle, J. W.  1971.  A Fenian Protestant in Canada:
Robert Lindsay Crawford, 1919-22.  Canadian Historical Review. 52:2:165-175.

Brady, A.  1925.  Thomas D'Arcy McGee.  The Macmillan Co. of Canada, Ltd., Toronto.

Brebner, J. B. 1945. The North Atlantic Triangle. Yale Univ., New Haven.

Brock, D. J. 1969. Richard Talbot, The Tipperary Irish and the Formative Years of London Township. Univ. Western Ontario. Masters thesis.

Browne, P. W. 1933. Some Irish Leaders in Canada. Studies: An Irish Quart. Rev. 22:245-256.

Brusher, J. S. 1943. The Fenian Invasions of Canada. St. Louis Univ. Ph.D. dissertation.

Bull, W. P. 1936. From Boyne to Brampton: John the Orangeman at Home and Abroad. McLeod, Toronto.

Burke, A. E. 1909-10. The Irishman's Place in the Empire. In: Empire Club of Canada Addresses 1909-10. Toronto. pp. 225-232.

Burns, R. B. 1966. A Critical Biography of Thomas D'Arcy McGee. McGill Univ. Ph.D. dissertation.

_____. 1970. D'Arcy McGee and the Fenians. In: Fenians and Fenianism. M. Harmon, ed., Univ. Washington, Seattle. pp. 77-92.

Callahan, J. M. 1896. The Northern Lake Frontier during the Civil War. Amer. Hist. Assn. Rpt. 1896:337-59.

Cameron, M. A. 1970. Fenian Times in Nova Scotia. Coll. Nova Scotia Hist. Soc. 37:103-152.

Cameron, W. 1976. Selecting Peter Robinson's Irish Emigrants. Soc. Hist. 9:29-46.

Campbell, F. W. 1904. The Fenian Invasions of Canada of 1866 and 1870. J. Lovell & Son, Montreal.

Clyne, H. R. N. 1964. Vancouvers 29th: A Chronicl of the 29th in Flanders Fields. Tebin's Tigers Assn Vancouver.

Coffey, A. 1933. A Bibliography of the Honorable Thomas D'Arcy McGee. McGill Univ. Library School, Montreal.

Conner, D. J. 1976. The Irish Canadians: Image and Self-Image. Univ. Brit. Columbia. Masters thesis.

Connolly, J. J. 1938-39. Lord Selkirks Efforts to Establish a Settlement for Irish Catholics at the Red River. Can. Cath. Hist. Assn. Report. 6th:39-49.

Cooper, J. A. 1897. The Fenian Raid of 1966. Can. Magz. 10:41-55.

Cooper. J. I. 1949. Quebec Ship Labourers Benevolent Society 1857-1888. Can. Hist. Rev. 30:4:336-343.

_____. 1955. Irish Immigration and the Canadian Church Before the Middle of the 19th Century. J. Can. Church Hist. Soc. 2:3:20.

Crawford, M. and K. Armstrong. 1970. The Fenians. Irwin Clarke, Toronto.

Cross, D. S. 1969. The Irish in Montreal 1867-1896. McGill Univ. Masters thesis.

Cross, M. 1973. The Shiner's War: Social Violence in the Ottawa Valley in the 1830's. Can. Hist. Rev. 15:1:1-26.

Cruikshank, E. A. 1926. The Fenian Raid of 1866. WCHSPR 2:9-49.

Cumberland, B. 1910. The Fenian Raid of 1866 and Events on the Frontier. Proc. Transact. Ray Soc. Can. 4:85-108 (3rd series).

Dafoe, J. W. 1898. The Fenian Invasion of Quebec, 1966. Can. Magz. 10:339-47.

Davin, N. F. 1877. Irishman in Canada. Sampeon, Low, Marston, London.

_____. 1877. The Irishman in Canada. MacLean & Co., Toronto. (reprinted 1969, Irish Univ. Press).

Davis, H. A. 1955. The Fenian Raid on New Brunswick. Canadian Hist. Rev. 36:4:316-334.

Davis, R. 1973. Irish Catholics and the Manitoba School Crises 1885-1921. Eire-Ireland. 8:3:29-64.

Denison, G. T. 1866. History of the Fenian Raid on Fort Erie: With an Account of the Battle of Ridgeway. Rollo & Adam, Toronto.

Dillon, W. F. 1963. The Irish in London 1826-1861. McGill Univ. Masters thesis.

Dixon, G. T. 1892. The Archdiocese of Toronto and Bishop Walsh. Jubilee Volume, Toronto.

Doharty, E. J. 1976. An Analysis of Social and Political Thought in the Irish Canadian Press in Upper Canada 1858-1867. Univ. Waterloo. Masters thesis.

Donovan, H. 1929-30. Fenian Memories in Northern New York. J. Amer. Irish Hist. Soc. 28:148-152.

Duncan, K. 1965. Irish Famine Immigration and the Social Structure of Canada West. Can. Rev. Socio. & Anthro. 2:1:19-40.

_____. 1968. Irish Famine Immigration and the Social Structure of Canada West. In: Canada: A Sociological Profile. W. E. Mann ed. MacMillan, Toronto. pp. 1-16.

Dunn, J. F. 1926. Recollections of the Battle of Ridgeway. WCHSPR 2:50-56.

Ellis, W. 1899. The Adventures of a Prisoner of War. Can. Magz. 13:199-203.

_____. 1926. The Adventures of a Prisoner of War in the Fenian Raid. Can. Def. Quart. 3:290-315.

Falconer, R.  1935.  Irish Influence on Higher Education in Canada.  Roy Soc. Canad. Proc. Series 3.  29:2:121-143.

Fazakas, R.  1977.  The Donnelly Album.  Macmillan, Toronto.

Fleming, J. C.  1877.  Orangeism and the 12th of July Riots in Montreal.  Fleming, Montreal.

Gallagher, J. A.  1935-36.  The Irish Emigration of 1847 and Its Canadian Consequences.  Can. Cath. Hist. Assn. Report.  1935-36:43-57.

Galvin, C.  1978.  The Holy Land: A History of Ennismore Township.  Township of Ennismore, Ennismore, Ontario.

Galvin, M. J.  Catholic Protestant Relations in Ontario 1864-1875.  Univ. Toronto.  Masters thesis.

Gauust, D.  1866.  History of the Fenian Invasion of Canada, W. Brown, Hamilton, Ontario.  (Real Name, W. Brown).

Gibbon, J. M.  1938.  Ireland and Canada.  In: Canadian Mosiac.  J. M. Gibbon, Toronto.  pp. 115-145.

Gibeault, J.  1971.  Les Relations Entre Thomas. D'Arcy McGee et. James Moylan, Editeur du Canadian Freeman 1858-1865.  Univ. Ottawa.  Masters thesis.

Gowan, O.  1974.  Orangeism and the Immigrant Question 1830-33.  Ontario History.  66:193-210.

Green, E. R.  1958.  The Fenians.  History Today.  8:689-705.

Gregg, G. R. and E. P. Roden.  1867.  Trials of the Fenian Prisoners at Toronto.  Leader Press, Toronto.

Guerin, T.  1946.  The Gael in New France, Montreal.

Guillett, E. C.  1937.  The Great Migration.  Nelson, Toronto.

_____. ed. 1956. Documents Relative to the Peter Robinson Emigration of 1825. Peterborough Public Library, Peterborough, Ontario.

Hamilton, C. F. 1929. The Canadian Militia: The Fenian Raids. Can. Def. Quart. 6:344-353, 474-483.

_____. 1929. The Canadian Militia: The Fenian Raids. Can. Def. Quart. 7:78-89.

Helm, M. 1970. Civil Disorders in Biddulph Township, 1850-1880. Sir George Williams Univ. Thesis equivalent.

Hickey, W. 1831. Hints on Emigration to Upper Canada. W. C. Curry, Dublin.

Hodgins, J. G. 1875. Irishmen in Canada: Their Union Not Inconsistent with the Development of Canadian National Feeling. Lovell Bros., Toronto.

Hogan, B. F. 1978. Current Bibliography of Canadian Church History. Can. Cath. Hist. Assoc. 45:101-141.

Horall, S. W. 1966. Canada and the Irish Question: A Study of the Canadian Response to Home Rule 1882-1893. Carleton Univ. Masters thesis.

Hoslett, S. D. 1940. The Fenian Brotherhood. Americana. 34:596-613.

Houston, C. and W. J. Smyth. 1978. The Orange Order and the Expansion of the Frontier in Ontario, 1830-1900. J. Hist. Geog. 4:3:251-264.

Hunter, C. 1911. Reminiscences of the Fenian Raid. Niagra Hist. Soc. 20:3-22.

Hurst, J. W. 1969. The Fenians: A Bibliography, Eire/Ireland. 4:4:90-106.

Isham, C. 1887. The Fishery Question: Its Origin, History and Present Situation. G. P. Putman's Sons, New York.

Jackson, R. W. 1948. Ancient Ireland and its Links with Canada. Canadian Geographical Journal. 36:4:172-179.

Jameson, A. 1923. Winter Studies and Summer Rambles in Canada. McCleland-Stewart, Toronto.

Jenkins, B. 1968. The British Government, Sir John A. Macdonald and the Fenian Claims. Canadian Historical Review 49:2:142-159.

Johnson, J. K. 1966. Colonel James Fitzgibbon and the Suppression of Irish Riots in Upper Canada. Ontario Hist. 58:3:139-155.

Johnson, R. P. 1952. The Fenian Invasion of 1871. Hist. Soc. Manitoba Ser. III, No. 7:30-39.

Katz, M. B. and I. E. Davey. n.d. Youth and Early Industrialization in a Canadian City. In: Turning Points. J. Demos and S. S. Bocock eds. Univ. Chicago. pp. S81-S119.

Kealy, G. S. 1976. The Orange Order in Toronto: Religious Riot and the Working Class. In: G. S. Kealy and P. Warrian, eds. Essays in Canadian Working Class History, Toronto. pp. 13-14.

Keep, G. R. C. 1945. The Irish Migration to Montreal 1847-1867. McGill Univ. Masters thesis.

_____. 1950. The Irish Adjustment in Montreal 1847-1807. Can. Hist. Rev. 31:1:39-46.

_____. 1951. The Irish Migration to North America in the 2nd Half of the 19th Century. Univ. Dublin. Ph.D. dissertation.

_____. 1953. A Canadian Emigration Commissioner in Northern Ireland. Canadian Historical Journal. 34:2:151-157.

_____. 1956. Irish Migration to Montreal, 1847-1867. Canadian Studies Series No. 19. Univ. of Rochester, New York.

Kelley, T. P. 1954. The Black Donnellys. Greywood, Winnipeg.

Kelly, E. T. 1967. Coming of the New Foundland Irish: State of the Question. Newfoundland Quart. 65:18-20, 66:14-16.

Kerr, W. 1942. When Orange and Green United 1832-39: The Alliance of Macdonnell and Gowan. Ontario Hist. Soc. Papers and Records. 34:34-42.

Kilfoil, W. P. 1962. Johnville: The Centennial Story of an Irish Settlement. Unipress, Fredericton.

King, C. L. 1909. The Fenian Movement. Univ. Colo. Stud. 6:187-213.

Larmour, R. 1898. Personel Reminiscences of the Fenian Raid of June, 1866. Can. Magz. 10:121-127.

Liguori, M. 1961. The Impact of a Century of Irish Catholic Immigration in Nova Scotia 1750-1850. Univ. of Ottawa. Ph.D. dissertation.

Luthart, T. 1965. An Examination of the Fenian Movement with Emphasis on the Role of Buffalo. SUNY at Buffalo. Masters thesis.

Lyne, D. C. 1960. The Irish in the Province of Canada 1850-67. McGill Univ. Masters thesis.

MacDonald, J. A. 1910. Troublous Times in Canada: A History of the Fenian Raids of 1866 and 1870. W. S. Johnston & Co., Toronto.

MacDougall, P. 1870. The Fenian Raid and the Colonial Office. Blackwood's Magz. 108:493-508.

Mackinnon, I. n.d. Settlement and Churches in Nova Scotia 1749-1776. Walker Press, Montreal.

Mahoney, T. H. D. 1956. Mr. Burke's Imperial Mentality and the Proposed Irish Absentee Tax of 1773. Canadian Hist. Rev. 37:2:158-166.

Mannion, J. J. 1971. Irish Imprints on the Land-
scape of Eastern Canada in the 19th Century. Univ.
Toronto. Ph.D. dissertation.

_____. 1974. Irish Settlements in Eastern
Canada: Study of Cultural Transfer and Adaptation.
Univ. of Toronto, Toronto.

Maltby, P. L. and M. Maltby. 1963. New Look at
the Peter Robinson Emigration of 1823. Ontario
Hist. 55:15-21.

Martell, J. S. 1938. Military Settlements in Nova
Scotia After the War of 1812. Collections of the
Nova Scotia Hist. Soc. Vol. 24.

_____. 1942. Immigration to and Emigration from
Nova Scotia 1815-1838. Halifax Public Archives of
Nova Scotia Press, Pub. No. 6.

Maurault, O. 1922. La Congregation Irlandaise de
Montreal. Rev. Trimestriele Canada. 8:267-290.

McCallum, R. H. 1915. Experiences of a Queen's
Own Rifleman at Ridgeway. Waterloo Hist. Soc. Rpt.
3:24-29.

McGee, R. F. 1967. The Fenian Raids on the Huntington Frontiers 1866 and 1870. Huntington, Quebec.

_____. 1969. The Toronto Irish Catholic Press
and Fenianism, 1863-66. Univ. of Ottawa. Masters
thesis.

McGee, T. D. 1858. Canadian Ballads and Occasional
Verses. J. Lovell, Montreal.

_____. 1866. The Irish Position in British and
in Republican North America. M. Longmore, Montreal.

McMicken, G. 1888. The Abortive Fenian Raid on
Manitoba. Hist. & Sci. Soc., Manitoba, Transaction
No. 32.

McMurray, E. J. 1925. Thomas D'Arcy McGee. In: Empire Club of Canada Addresses. Toronto. pp. 167-179.

Missiquoi County Hist. Soc. 1967. The Fenian Raids, 1866-1870. Missiquoi County Hist. Soc., Stanbridge East, Quebec.

Mitchell, J. 1970. The Yellow Briar: A Story of the Irish on the Canadian Countryside by Patrick Slater. Macmillan, Toronto.

Morehouse, F. 1928. Canadian Migration in the Forties. Can. Hist. Rev. 9:309-329.

Morse, S. L. 1946. Immigration to Nova Scotia 1839-1851. Dalhousie Univ. Masters thesis.

Mullally, E. J. 1838-39. The Hon. Edward Whelan: A Father of Confederation from Prince Edward Island -- One of Ireland's Gifts to Canada. Can. Cath. Hist. Assn. Rpt. 67-84.

Murphy, C., ed. 1937. Thomas D'Arcy McGee 1825-1925: A Collection of Speeches and Addresses. Macmillan, Toronto.

Nicolson, M. 1976. The Irish Catholics in Toronto 1840-1900. Univ. Guelph. Ph.D. dissertation.

Niedhardt, W. S. 1967. The Fenian Brotherhood and Southwestern Ontario. Univ. West. Ontario. Masters thesis.

_____. 1968. The Fenian Brotherhood and West Ontario: The Final Years. Ontario Hist. 60:149-161.

_____. 1969. The Abortive Fenian Uprising in Canada West: A Document Study. Ontario Hist. 61:74-76.

_____. 1972. The Fenian Brotherhood and its Role in Canadian History. The York Pioneer. 1972:2-13.

_____. 1973. We've Nothing Else To Do: The Fenian Invasion of Canada, 1866. Canada: Amer. Hist. Magz. 1:2:1-19.

_____. 1974. The Fenian Trials in the Province of Canada, 1866-67: A Case Study of Law and Politics in Action. Ontario. Hist. 66:1:23-36.

_____. 1975. Fenianism in North America. Penna. St. Univ., State College, Pennsylvania.

Nolte, W. M. 1975. The Irish in Canada 1815-1867. Univ. Maryland. Ph.D. dissertation.

O'Brien, C. 1894. Memoirs of Ft. Rev. Edmund Burke, Thorburn, Ottawa.

O'Brien, J. 1884. Irish Celts: A Cyclopedia of Race History. L. F. Kilroy, Detroit.

O'Brien, W. 1897. Was Fenianism Ever Formidable? Contemp. Rev. 71:680-93.

O'Dwyer, G. F. 1928. Irish Soldiers at the Seige of Louisburgh, Nova Scotia. J. Amer. Irish Hist. Soc. 27:278-284.

O'Farrell, J. 1930. Irish Families in Ancient Quebec Records, With Some Account of Soldiers From the Irish Brigade Regiments of France Serving With the Army of Montcalm. J. Amer. Irish. Hist. Soc. 28:157-172.

O'Hagan, T. 1900. The Catholic Church in Ontario. Amer. Cath. Quart. Rev. 15:15-30.

O'Hanly, J. L. P. 1872. The Political Standing of Irish Catholics in Canada. J. L. O'Hanly, Ottawa.

O'Neill, P. 1975. The Oldest City: The Story of St. Johns Newfoundland. Press Porcepic, Erin, Ontario.

Ormsby, M. A. 1950. Some Irish Figures in Colonial Days. Brit. Columbia Hist. Quart. 1950:61-82.

Pammett, H. T.   1936.   Assisted Emigration from Ireland to Upper Canada.   Under Peter Robinson in 1825.   Ontario Hist. Soc. Papers and Records. 31:178-214.

Parr, G. J.   1974.   The Welcome and the Wake: Attitudes in Canada West Toward Irish Famine Migration.   Ontario Hist. 66:101-113.

Pendle, F. E., Jr.   1980.   Land Settlement and Development Problems in Southwestern Upper Canada 1791-1867.   Kent State Univ.   Ph.D. dissertation.

Phelan, J.   1951.   The Ardent Exile.   Macmillan Co. of Canada, Toronto.

Phillips, R. C.   1911-12.   The Irishman as an Empire Builder.   In:   Empire Club of Canada Addresses 48-56, Toronto.

Poole, T. W.   1867.   The Early Settlement of Peterborough County.   Peterborough Printing Co., Peterborough.   (reprinted, 1967).

Pritchett, J. P.   1929.   The Origins of the So-Called Fenian Raid on Manitoba in 1871.   Can. Hist. Rev. 10:1:23-42.

_____.   ed.   1930.   Letter from W. B. O'Donoghue to Jay Cooke March 29, 1871 About the Scheme for the Annexation of Ruperts Land.   North Dakota Hist. Quart. 5:49-53.

Proudfoot, A. B.   1970.   Irish Settlers in Alberta. Ulster Folklife. 15/16:216-223.

Prowse, D. W.   1895.   A History of Newfoundland from the English, Colonial, and Foreign Records.   Macmillan and Co., New York and London.

Punch, T.   1975.   The Irish Community of Halifax 1815-1867.   Dalhousie Univ.   Ph.D. dissertation.

Quealy, F. M.   1961.   The Fenian Invasion of Canada West.   Ontario Hist. 53:37-66.

Ray, P. G. 1924. Un Irlandais a'Quebec en 1687. Bull. Researchers Hist. 30:385-388.

Raymond, W. O. 1912. Col. Alexander McNutt and the Pre-Loyalist Settlements of Nova Scotia. Royal. Soc. Can. Proc. Sect. 11:23.

Reavley, A. W. 1926. Personal Experiences in the Fenian Raid. WCHSPR 2:66-74.

Rivet, M. 1969. Les Irlandis a'Quebec, 1870-1968. Laval Univ. Masters thesis.

Saunders, L. H. n.d. The Story of Orangeism, its Origin and History for More Than a Century and a Quarter in Canada, Particularly in Ontario West. Grand Orange Lodge of Ontario-West, Toronto.

_____. n.d. The Cost of Romanism to the Nation and the Truth About Quebec's Part in the Second World War. Britannia Pub., Toronto.

Senior, H. 1967. Quebec and the Fenians. Can. Hist. Rev. 48:1:26-44.

_____. 1968. The Genesis of Canadian Orangeism. Ontario Hist. 60:2:13-29.

_____. 1972. Orangeism, the Canadian Phase. McGraw-Hill, Toronto.

_____. 1974. Ogle Gowan, Orangeism and the Immigrant Question, 1830-1833. Ontario Hist. 66: 193-210.

_____. 1978. The Fenians and Canada. Macmillan, Toronto.

Severance, F. H. 1921. The Fenian Raid of 1866. Buffalo Hist. Soc. 25:263-285.

Sheehy, M. 1945. The Irish in Quebec. Can. Cath. Hist. Assn. Rpt. 1943-1944:212.

Shrive, F. M. 1959. Charles Mann: A Document on
the Red River Rebellion. Can. Hist. Rev. 40:218-226.

Sifton, C. 1956. The Sifton Family Record. Sifton
Family Assn. Toronto.

Skelton, I. 1925. The Life of Thomas D'Arcy McGee.
The Garden City Press, Gardenvale, Quebec.

Slattery. T. P. 1968. The Assassination of D'Arcy
McGee. Doubleday, Toronto.

Sommerville, A. 1866. Narrative of the Fenian
Invasion of Canada. Hamilton, Ontario.

Stacey, C. P. 1931. Fenianism of the Rise of
National Feeling in Canada at the Time of Confederation. Can. Hist. Rev. 12:3:238-261.

_____. 1933. The Garrison of Fort Wellington:
A Military Dispute During the Fenian Troubles. Can.
Hist. Rev. 14:2:161-176.

_____. 1934. A Fenian Interlude: The Story of
Michael Murphy. Can. Hist. Rev. 15:2:133-154.

_____. 1935. The Fenian Troubles and Canadian
Military Development. 1865-1871. Rpt. Ann. Mtg.
Can. Hist. Assn. 26-35.

_____. 1936. The Withdrawal of the Imperial
Garrison from Newfoundland, 1870. Can. Hist. Rev.
17:2:147-158.

Stanley, G. F. G. 1963-1964. L'Invasion Fenienne
Au Manitoba. Rev. d'Historique de L'Amerique
Francaise. 17:258-268.

Stock, G. 1962. The Irish Catholics of Sadbury,
Ontario 1883-1930. Univ. West. Ontario. Masters
thesis.

Stewart, H. L. 1949. The Irish in Nova Scotia:
Annals of the Charitable Irish Society of Halifax
(1786-1836). Kentville Publ. Co., Kentville, N.S.

148

Stortz, G. J.  1979.  Irish Immigration in the
Nineteenth Century.  The Immigration History Newsletter.  11:2:9-14.

Sweeny, W. M.  1924.  The Fenian Invasion of Canada,
1866.  J. Amer. Irish Hist. Soc. 23:193-203.

Taylor, J. M.  1978.  Fenian Raids Against Canada.
Amer. Hist. Illus. 13:5:32-39.

Tepperman, L.  1974.  Ethnic Variations in Marriage
and Fertility Canada 1871.  Can. Rev. Socio. and
Anthro. 11:4:324-343.

Toner, P.  1971.  The Military Organization of the
Canadian Fenians 1886-1870.  The Irish Sword. 10:
38-44.

de Tremaudan, A. H.  1923.  Louis Riel and the
Fenian Raid of 1871.  Can. Hist. Rev. 4:2:132-144.

Tucker, G.  1930-31.  The Famine Immigration to
Canada, 1847.  Amer. Hist. Rev. 36:3:533-549.

Vesey, M.  1939.  When New Brunswick Suffered Invasion.  Dalhousie Rev. 19:197-204.

Vroom, J.  1898.  The Fenians on the St. Croix.
Can. Magz. 10:411-413.

Walker, M. G.  1929.  The Fenian Movement 1858-1872.
Ohio State Univ.  Ph.D. dissertation.

Watt, J. T.  1967.  Anti-Catholic Nativism in Canada:
The Protestant Protective Association.  Can. Hist.
Rev. 48:45-58.

Wells, G.  1926.  A Romance of the Raid.  WCHSPR
2:80-81.

_____.  1926.  The Fenian Raid in Willoughby.
WCHSPR 2:57-59.

Wheeler, A. E.  1931.  Reminiscences of the Fenian
Raids of 66.  York Pioneer and Hist. Soc. Ann. Rpt.
1930:15-19.

Wilson, E. C. 1961. The Impact of a Century of Irish Catholic Immigration in Nova Scotia (1750-1850). Univ. Ottawa. Ph.D. dissertation.

Wilson, P. 1936. Irish John Wilson and Family, Loyalists. Ontario Hist. Soc. Papers and Records. 31:228-242.

Woodcock, G. 1967. The Confederation of Canada. History Today. 18:386-392.

_____. 1967. The Confederation of Canada, Part II. History Today. 18:437-443.

Woodland, L. A. 1973. Ottawa Irish 1825-1870: A Study in Acculturation. Univ. Brit. Columbia. Ph.D. dissertation.

Chapter 11: THE IRISH IN NEW ENGLAND

Ackland, T. 1907. The Celts of Colonial Boston. J. Amer. Irish Hist. Soc. 7:80-95.

Anderson, G. T. 1944. The Slavery Issue as a Factor in Massachusetts Politics From the Compromise of 1850 to the Outbreak of the Civil War. Univ. Chicago. Ph.D. dissertation.

Bean, W. G. 1934. Puritan Versus Celt, 1850-1860. New Engl. Quart. 7:70-89.

Brayley, A. W. 1889. The Complete History of the Boston Fire Department, Boston.

Brennan, J. F. 1910. The Irish Settlers of New Hampshire. J. Amer. Irish Hist. Soc. 9:247-257.

Carroll, L. F. 1969. Irish and Italians in Providence, Rhode Island, 1880-1960. Rhode Island Hist. 28:67-74.

Cole, D. B. 1963. Immigrant City: Lawrence Massachusetts. 1845-1921. Univ. North Carolina, Chapel Hill, North Carolina.

_____. 1963. The Shanty Irish, 1850-1865. In: D. B. Cole. Immigrant City Univ. of North Carolina Chapel Hill. pp. 27-41.

Cornwell, E. E., Jr. 1960. Party Absorption of Ethnic Groups: The Case of Providence, Rhode Island. Social Forces. 38:205-210.

Cosgrove, J. I. 1910. The Irish in Rhode Island, To and Including the Revolution. J. Amer. Irish Hist. Soc. 9:365-385.

Conley, P. T. and M. J. Smith. 1976. Catholicism in Rhode Island: The Formative Era. Rhode Island Bicentennial Foundation, Providence, Rhode Island.

Cullen, J. B., ed. 1889. The Story of the Irish in Boston. Cullen, Boston.

151

Cunningham, P. 1976. Irish Catholics in a Yankee Town: A Report About Brattheboro 1847-1898. Vermont Hist. 44:4:189-197.

Darling, A. B. 1924. Jacksonian Democracy in Massachusetts, 1824-1848. American Historical Review. 29:2:271-287.

Donovan, G. F. 1930. The Irish in Massachusetts Before 1700. Hist. Bulletin. 8:43-45, 53.

_____. 1931. The Pre-Revolutionary Irish in Massachusetts, 1620-1675. Geo Banta, Menasha, Wisconsin.

_____. 1931. The Pre-Revolutionary Irish in Massachusetts, 1620-1775. St. Louis Univ. Ph.D. dissertation.

_____. 1932. The Pre-Revolutionary Irish in Massachusetts, 1620-1775. Published by F. F. Donovan, Webster Groves, Missouri.

Driscoll, J. 1939. Background Paper on the Irish in Bridgeport, Connecticut. WPA Federal Writers Project.

Dubnoff, S. J. 1976. The Family and Absence from Work: Irish Workers in Lowell, Massachusetts. Cotton Mill, 1860. Brandeis Univ. Ph.D. dissertatio

Dubovik, P. N. 1975. Housing in Holyoke and its Effects on Family Life 1800-1910. Hist. J. West. Mass. 4:1:40-50.

Eisinger, P. K. 1978. Ethnic Political Transition in Boston, 1884-1933. Pol. Sci. Quart. 93:2:217-239.

Feinstein, E. F. 1973. Stamford in the Gilded Age. The Stamford Historical Society, Stamford.

Forbes, H. A. and H. Lee. 1967. Massachusetts Help to Ireland During the Great Famine. Forbes House, Milton, Massachusetts.

Frisch, M. H. 1969. The Community Elite and the Emergence of Urban Politics, Springfield, Massachusetts, 1840-1880. In: S. Thernstrom and R. Sennett. Nineteenth-Century Cities. Yale Univ., New Haven. pp. 277-296.

Fuchs, L. H. 1957. Presidential Politics in Boston: The Irish Response to Stevenson. New Eng. Quart. 30:435-447.

Gabriel, R. A. 1969. Ethnic Voting in Primary Elections: The Irish and Italians of Providence, Rhode Island. Bureau of Government Research, Kingston, Rhode Island.

Gearan, M. M. 1932. The Early Irish Settlers in the Town of Gardiner, Massachusetts. Fitchburg, Massachusetts.

Green, M. B. 1966. The Problem of Boston. Norton, New York.

Hale, R. W., Jr. 1957. American and Irish Revolutions. Mass. Hist. Soc. Proc. 70:50-55.

Handlin, O. 1959. Boston's Immigrants: A Study in Acculturation. Harvard Univ. Cambridge, Massachusetts.

Hareven, T. K. and M. Vinovskis. 1975. Marital Fertility, Ethnicity and Occupation in Urban Families: An Analysis of South Boston and the South End in 1880. J. Urban History. 1:293-315.

Hansen, M. L. 1929. The Second Colonization of New England. New Eng. Quart. 2:4:539-560.

Hunter, R. J. 1971. Dublin to Boston, 1719. Eire/Ireland. 6:2:18-24.

Jacobus, D. L. 1936. Irish in New England Before 1700. New Eng. Hist. and Geneological Register. 90:165-167.

Jeffrey-Jones, R. 1975. Massachusetts Labor and the League of Nation Controversy in 1919. Irish Hist. Studies. 19:76:396-416.

Kennedy, R. J. 1952. Single or Triple Melting Pot. Intermarriage in New Haven 1870-1950. Amer. J. Soc. 58:1:56.

Knights, P. 1971. The Plain People of Boston, 1830-1860: A Study in City Growth. Oxford Univ., New York.

Lankevich, G. J., ed. 1974. Boston: Chronological and Documentary History 1602-1970. Oceana, New York.

Lapomarda, V. 1970. Maurice Joseph Tobin: The Decline of Bossism in Boston. New England Quart. 43:365-366.

Lee, T. Z. 1916. The Irish of the Rhode Island Colony in Peace and War. J. Amer. Irish Hist. Soc. 15:156-167.

Linehan, J. C. 1906. Irish Pioneers in Boston and Vicinity. J. Amer. Hist. Soc. 6:75-84.

McKenna, J. J. 1950. Early Scotch-Irish and Irish in Berks. Hist. Rev. Berks Co. 1730-1898. Berks County, Pennsylvania.

Merwick, D. 1973. Boston Priests 1848-1910: A Study of Social and Intellectual Change. Harvard, Cambridge, Massachusetts.

Mitchell, A. G., Jr. 1976. Irish Family Patterns in 19th Century Ireland and Lowell, Massachusetts. Boston Univ. Ph.D. dissertation.

Morgan, J. H. 1975. The Irish of South Boston. World View. 18:6:24-27.

_____. 1978. Ethnoconsciousness and Political Powerlessness: Boston's Irish. Social Science. 53:159-167.

Morgan, M. and H. H. Gordon. 1979. Immigrant Families in an Industrial City: A Study of Households in Holyoke, 1880. J. Family History. 4:1: 59-68.

Mulkern, J. R. 1963. The Know-Nothing Party in Massachusetts. Boston Univ. Ph.D. dissertation.

Noonan, C. J. 1938. Nativism in Connecticut 1829-1860. Catholic Univ., Washington, D.C.

O'Beirne, J. 1960. Some Early Irish in Vermont. Vermont History. 28:63-72.

O'Brien, M. J. 1911. The Early Irish in Maine. J. Amer. Irish Hist. Soc. 10:162-170.

_____. 1913. The Lost Town of Cork, Maine. J. Amer. Irish Hist. Soc. 12:175-184.

_____. 1914. Irish Immigrants to New England. J. Amer. Irish Hist. Soc. 13:177-190.

_____. 1916. The Story of Old Leary Street or Cortland Street - The Leary Family in Early New York Hist. J. Amer. Irish Hist. Soc. 15:112-117.

_____. 1916. Some Stray Historical Nuggets from the Early Records of Massachusetts Towns. J. Amer. Irish Hist. Soc. 15:172-190.

_____. 1917. Early Irish Schoolmasters in New England. Cath. Hist. Rev. 3:52-71.

_____. 1918. Irish Mariners in New England. J. Amer. Irish Hist. Soc. 17:149-190.

_____. 1919. An Authorative Account of the Earliest Irish Pioneers in New England. J. Amer. Irish Hist. Soc. 18:110-144.

_____. 1919. Some Irish Names Culled from the Official Records of New Hampshire. J. Amer. Irish Hist. Soc. 18:176-181.

_____. 1919. Some Traces of the Irish Settlers in the Colony of Massachusetts Bay. J. Amer. Irish Hist. Soc. 18:145-162.

_____. 1919. Stray Historical Items from the Green Mountain State. J. Amer. Irish Hist. Soc. 18:182-186.

_____. 1919. The McCarthys in Early American History. Dodd and Mead, New York.

_____. 1921. An Authoritative Account of the Earliest Irish Pioneers in New England. J. Amer. Irish Hist. Soc. 18:110-444.

_____. 1922. The Kellys, Burkes and Sheas of the Massachusetts Line. J. Amer. Irish Hist. Soc. 21:107-110.

_____. 1923. The Connecticut Irish in the Revolution, Numerous Celtic Names Listed in the Muster Roles. J. Amer. Irish Hist. Soc. 22:196-214.

_____. 1925. Irish Settlers in Connecticut in the 17th and 18th Century. J. Amer. Irish Hist. Soc. 24:125-141.

_____. 1926. Irish Pioneers in New Hampshire. J. Amer. Irish Hist. Soc. 25:62-89.

_____. 1926. Obituary Notices in the Providence, Rhode Island, Newspapers. J. Amer. Irish Hist. Soc. 25:116-124.

_____. 1927. Early Irish Settlers in the Champlain Valley. Recorder. 4:1-4.

_____. 1927. John McCurdy: Irish Pioneer in Connecticut. J. Amer. Irish Hist. Soc. 26:199-200.

_____. 1927. The Pioneer Irish of Essex County, Massachusetts. J. Amer. Irish Hist. Soc. 26:137-149.

_____. 1937. Pioneer Irish in New England. P. J. Kenedy, New York.

O'Connell, W. H.  1960.  Early Years in Lowell.  In: Essays in the American Catholic Tradition.  P. A. Duhamel, Ed.  Rhinehart, New York.

O'Connor, T. H.  1979.  The Irish in Boston.  Urban and Social Change Rev. 12:2:19-23.

O'Dwyer, G. F.  1917.  Early Irish Names on the Ipswich (Massachusetts) Vital Records - 17th and 18th Century.  J. Amer. Irish Hist. Soc. 16:4:264-283.

_____.  1919.  Historical Gleanings from Massachusetts Records.  J. Amer. Irish Hist. Soc. 18:216-223.

_____.  1920.  Captain James Howard, Col. William Lithgow, Col. Arthur Noble and Other Irish Pioneers of Maine.  J. Amer. Irish Hist. Soc. 19:71-88.

_____.  1920.  Irish in Ipswich 1630-1700.  The Catholic World. 115:805-814.

_____.  1920.  Irish Names in New England Records.  J. Amer. Irish Hist. Soc. 19:89-91.

_____.  1920.  The Irish Catholic Genesis of Lowell.  Sullivan Brothers, Lowell, Massachusetts.

O'Malley, C. J.  1925.  American Irish Progress in Boston.  J. Irish Amer. Hist. Soc. 24:183-190.

Powers, V. E.  1976.  Invisible Immigrants the Pre-Famine Irish Community in Worcestor, Massachusetts 1826-1860.  Clark Univ.  Ph.D. dissertation.

Pryor, E. T., Jr.  1972.  Rhode Island Family Structure 1875 and 1960.  In:  Household and Family in Past Time.  P. Laslett and R. Walls, eds.  Cambridge Univ., Cambridge.  pp. 521-589.

Purcell, R. J.  1934.  Irish Colonists in Colonial Maryland.  Studies: Amer. Irish Quart. Rev. 23:279-294.

_____. 1934. Rhode Island's Early Schools and Irish Teachers. Cath. Educ. Rev. 32:402-415.

_____. 1934. Schools and Early Irish Teachers in New Hampshire. Cath. Educ. Rev. 32:608-718.

_____. 1935. Education and Irish Schoolmasters in Colonial Massachusetts. Cath. Educ. Rev. 33:467-479.

_____. 1935. Irish Builders of Colonial Rhode Island Studies. In: Irish Quart. Rev. 24:289-300.

_____. 1935. Maine: Early Schools and Irish Teachers. Cath. Educ. Rev. 33:211-225.

_____. 1935. Vermont: Schools and Early Irish Teachers. Cath. Educ. Rev. 33:277-281.

Quirk, R. D. 1936. The Irish Element in New Hampshire to 1805. Catholic Univ. Masters thesis.

Russell, F. 1964. The Great Interlude. McGraw-Hill, New York.

Ryan, D. P. 1979. Beyond the Ballot Box: A Social History of the Boston Irish 1845-1917. Univ. Massachusetts. Ph.D. dissertation.

Solomon, B. 1956. Ancestors and Immigrants: A Changing New England Tradition. Harvard, Cambridge.

Spofford, H. P. 1881. The Servant Girl Question. Houghton Mifflin, Boston (report, 1977 Arno Press, New York).

Stegner, W. 1944. Who Persecutes Boston? Atlantic. 174:45-52.

Sullivan, W. B. 1913. Celtic Danvers. Danvers Hist. Soc. Coll. 1:74-86.

Sweeney, K. 1976. Rum, Romanism Representations and Reform: Coalition Politics in Massachusetts, 1847-1853. Civil War Hist. 22:116-137.

Thernstrom, S. 1964. Poverty and Progress. Harvard Univ., Cambridge, Massachusetts.

_____. 1969. Immigrants and Wasps: Ethnic Differences in Occupational Mobility in Boston 1890-1940. In: S. Thernstrom and R. Sennett. Nineteenth-Century Cities. Yale Univ., New Haven. pp. 125-164.

_____. 1970. Irish Life in Yankee City. In: Catholicism in America. P. Gleason ed. Harper & Row, New York. pp. 58-64.

_____. 1973. The Other Bostonians: Poverty and Progress in an American Metropolis 1860-1970. Harvard, Cambridge.

Toomey, J. J. and E. P. B. Ranking. 1901. History of South Boston. Published by authors, Boston.

Towne, W. H. and M. J. O'Brien. 1919. Early Irish Settlers at Worcester, Massachusetts. J. Amer. Irish Hist. Soc. 18:169-175.

Walsh, M. E. 1937. The Irish in Rhode Island from 1800 to 1865. Catholic Univ. Masters thesis.

Ward, D. 1963. Nineteenth Century Boston: A Study in the Role of Antecendant and Adjacent Conditions in the Spatial Aspects of Urban Growth. Univ. Wisconsin. Ph.D. dissertation.

Wessel, B. B. 1931. An Ethnic Survey of Woonsocket, Rode Island. Univ. of Chicago, Chicago.

Wheeler, R. A. 1973. Fifth Ward Irish-Immigrant Mobility in Providence 1850-1870. Rhode Island Hist. 32:53-61.

White, A. O. 1973. Antebellum School Reform in Boston: Integrationists and Separatists. Phylon. 34:203-218.

Whyte, W. F. 1939. Race Conflicts in the North end of Boston from 1860 to the present. New Eng. Quart. 12:623-642.

Wood, G. 1960. Massachusetts Mugwumps, New Eng.
Quart. 33:435-451.

Woods, R. A. 1899. Irish in Boston. In: City
Wilderness. R. A. Woods ed. Houghton, Boston.

_____. 1902. Irish in Boston. In: Americans
in Process. R. A. Woods ed. Houghton, Boston.

Zolot, H. M. 1975. The Issue of Good Government
and James Michael Curley: Curley and the Boston
Scene from 1897-1918. State Univ. of New York.
Stoney Brook. Ph.D. dissertation.

Chapter 12:   THE IRISH IN NEW YORK AND THE MIDDLE
              ATLANTIC STATES

Albion, R. G.  1939.  The Rise of the Port of New
York 1815-1860.  Scribners, New York.

Alfred, W.  1971.  Ourselves Alone Irish Exiles in
Brooklyn.  The Atlantic.  227:3:53-58.

Allison, M. M.  1952.  IFFLY: "Ghost Town."  West
Pa. Hist. Magz.  35:93-102.

Anon.  1853.  St. Nicholas and Five Points.  Putnams
Magz.  1:509-512.

_____.  1902.  Lists of Servants Who Sailed from
Dublin 1746-47 on the Euryal and Arrived in Philadelphia. Pennsylvania Magz. Hist. and Biog. 26:287.

_____.  1912.  The Irish Settlement in the Forks
of the Delaware.  Penna. Germania, N. S. 1:632-640.

_____.  1926.  Irish Names in Early Admiralty
Litigation in New York.  Recorder.  3:17-19.

Anspach, M. R.  1954.  The Molly Maguires in the
Anthracite Coal Regions of Pennsylvania.  1850-1890.
Now and Then.  11:25-34.

Aurand, H. W.  1968.  The Anthracite Strike of 1887-
1888.  Penna. Hist.  35:172-173.

Bannan, T.  1911.  Pioneer Irish of Onondaga, About
1776-1847.  G. P. Putnam, New York.

Barrett, J. P.  1970.  The Life and Death of an Irish
Neighborhood.  Phila. Magz.  61:3:85-87, 128-263.

_____.  1975.  The Sesqui-Centennial History of
St. Denis Parish.  St. Denis Parish, Havertown, Pennsylvania.

Bayor, R. H.  1978.  Neighbors in Conflict:  The
Irish, Germans, Jews and Italians of New York City
1929-1941.  Johns Hopkins, Baltimore.

Beadles, J. A. 1974. The Syracuse Irish 1812-1928: Immigration, Catholicism Socioeconomic Status, Politics and Irish Nationalism. Syracuse Univ. Ph.D. dissertation.

Bennett, W. H. 1909. Catholic Footsteps in Old New York. Schwartz, Kerwin & Fauss, New York.

_____. 1922. Some Pre-Civil War Irish Militiamen of Brooklyn, New York. J. Amer. Irish Hist. Soc. 21:172-180.

_____. 1927. Handbook to Catholic Historical New York City. Schwartz, Kerwin & Fauss, New York.

Berthoff, R. 1965. The Social Order of the Anthracite Region, 1825-1902. Penna. Magz. Hist. and Biog. 89:261-291.

Blumin, S. 1969. Mobility and Change in Antebellum Philadelphia. In: S. Thernstrom and R. Sennett, eds Nineteenth Century Cities. Yale Univ., New Haven. pp. 165-208.

Bodnar, J., ed. 1937. The Ethnic Experience in Philadelphia. Bucknell Univ. Press, Lewisburg, Pennsylvania.

Browne, P. W. 1934. Thomas Dongan: Soldier and Statesman Irish Catholic Governor of New York, 1683-1688. Studies: Amer. Irish Quart. Rev. 23:489-501.

Buckley, J. P. 1974. The New York Irish: Their View of American Foreign Policy, 1914-1921. New York Univ. Ph.D. dissertation. (reprinted, 1976, Arno).

Burke, O. 1959. New York Irish: Pictures Jubilee. 6:6-15.

Burstein, A. N. 1975. Residential Distribution and Mobility of Irish and German Immigrants in Philadelphia 1850-1880. Univ. Pennsylvania. Ph.D. dissertation.

Carter, E. C. 1970. A "Wild Irishman" Under Every Federalists Bed: Naturalization in Philadelphia, 1789-1806. Penna. Magz. Hist. Biog. 94:331-346.

Chalmers, L. 1968. Fernando Wood - Tamany Hall. New York Hist. Soc. Quart. 52:329-402.

Clark,D. J. 1971. A Pattern of Urban Growth, Residential Development and Church Location in Philadelphia. Rec. Amer. Cath. Hist. Soc. 82:159-170.

_____. 1971. Muted Heritage: Gaelic in an American City. Eire/Ireland. 6:1:3-7.

_____. 1972. Irish-American Presence. Ethnic Philadelphia. 3:1:3-4.

_____. 1972. Kellyville: Immigrant Enterprise. Penna. Hist. 39:1:40-49.

_____. 1973. The Philadelphia Irish: Persistent Presence. In: Peoples of Philadelphia. A. F. Davis and M. H. Haller, eds. Temple Univ., Philadelphia. pp. 135-154.

_____. 1974. The Irish in Philadelphia: Ten Generations of Urban Experience. Temple Univ., Philadelphia.

_____. 1977. Babes in Bondage: Indentured Irish Children in Philadelphia in the 19th Century. Penna. Magz. Hist. and Biog. 101:475-486.

Clark, D. J. 1970. The Adjustment of Irish Immigrants to Urban Life: The Philadelphia Experience, 1840-1870. Temple Univ. Ph.D. dissertation.

_____. 1971. Militants of the 1860's: The Philadelphia Fenians. Penna. Magz. Hist. and Biog. 95:98-108.

Coleman, J. W. 1936. The Molly Maguire Riots: Industrial Conflict in the Pennsylvania Coal Region. Garrett and Massie, Inc., Richmond, Virginia. (report, Arno Press, 1969).

Collins, C. W. 1974. Alexander Macomb. York State Tradition. 28:3:18-20.

Cook, A. 1974. The Armies of the Streets. The New York Draft Riots of 1863. Univ. Kentucky, Lexington.

Coyle, J. G. 1915. American Irish Governors of Pennsylvania. J. Amer. Irish Hist. Soc. 14:145-161.

Curran, T. J. 1963. Know Nothings of New York State. Columbia Univ. Ph.D. dissertation.

Davis, A. and M. Haller, eds. 1973. The Peoples of Philadelphia: A History of Ethnic Groups and Lower Class Life 1790-1940. Temple Univ., Pennsylvania.

Dolan, J. P. 1974. Immigrants in the City: New York Irish and German Catholics. Church History. 41:3:354-68.

Dolan, R. 1954. Matthew Carey, Citizen and Publisher Amer. Cath. Hist. Soc. Rec. 65:116-28.

Donovan, H. D. A. 1930. Fenian Memories in Northern New York. J. Amer. Irish Hist. Soc. 28:148-152.

Dowling, V. J. 1909. Irish Pioneers in New York. J. Amer. Irish Hist. Soc. 8:117-139.

Doyle, R. D. 1932. The Pre-Revolutionary Irish in New York, 1643-1775. St. Louis Univ. Ph.D. dissertation.

Dubnoff, S. J. 1976. The Family and Absence from Work: Irish Workers in Lowell, Massachusetts Cotton Mill, 1860. Brandeis Univ. Ph.D. dissertation.

Dunn, J. P. 1951. Between Riots in 1844. Amer. Cath. Hist. Soc. Rec. 62:64-65.

Eno, J. N. 1927. Irish Revolutionary Soldiers in New York State and Elsewhere. Americana. 21:631-638.

Ernst, R. 1948. Economic Nativism in New York City During the 1840's. New York Hist. 29:170-186.

_____. 1949.  Immigrant Life in New York City 1825-1863.  Kings Crown, New York.

Feldberg, M.  1974.  The Crowd in Philadelphia History:  A Comparative Perspective.  Labor History. 15:323-336.

_____. 1975.  The Philadelphia Riots of 1844: A Study of Ethnic Conflict.  Greenwood Press, Westport, New York.

Filler, Louis.  1954.  The Early Godkin.  Hist. 17:43-66.

Fitzpatrick, F. E.  1948.  Irish Immigration to New York from 1865-1880.  Catholic Univ. Washington. Masters thesis.

_____. 1948.  The Irish Immigration into New York from 1865-1880.  Columbia Univ.  Masters thesis.

Flynn, E. J.  1947.  Your the Boss:  New York. Viking, New York.

Foster, G. G.  1849.  New York in Slices:  By An Experienced Carver.  W. H. Graham, W. F. Burgess, New York.

Friel, B.  1965.  Philadelphia, Here I Come.  Farrar, Straus and Giroux, New York.

Garnery, W. P.  1973.  The Ethnic Factor in Erie Politics 1900-1970.  Univ. Pittsburgh.  Ph.D. dissertation.

Geffen, E. M.  1969.  Violence in Philadelphia in the 1840's and 1850's.  Penna. Hist. 36:4:381.

George, J. J.  1979.  Philadelphia Catholic Herald: The Civil War Years.  Pa. Magz. Hist. Biog. 103:2: 196-221.

Gerard, J.  1883.  The Impress of Nationalities Upon the City of New York.  Columbia Spectator, New York.

Gibbons, P. E.  1877.  The Miners of Scranton Pennsylvania.  Harpers New Monthly Magz. 15:916-927.

Gibson, F. E. 1951. The Attitudes of the New York Irish Toward State and National Affairs, 1848-1892. Columbia University Press, New York.

Glasco, L. A. 1973. Ethnicity and Social Structure: Irish, Germans, and Native-Born of Buffalo, New York, 1850-1860. SUNY at Buffalo. Ph.D. dissertation.

_____. 1975. The Life Cycles and Household Structures of American Ethnic Groups: Irish, German and Native-Born Whites in Buffalo, New York, 1885. J. Urban History. 1:338-364.

_____. 1977. Ethnicity and Occupation in Mid-Nineteenth Century: Irish, Germans and Native-Born Whites in Buffalo, New York. In: Immigrants in Industrial America, R. L. Ehrlich, ed. Univ. of Virginia, Charlottesville. pp. 150-175.

_____. 1977. The Life Cycles and Household Structure of American Ethnic Groups: Irish, Germans and Native-Born Whites. Buffalo, New York, 1855. In: T. K. Hareven, Family and Kin in Urban Communities 1700-1930. New Viewpoints, New York. pp. 122-143.

Good, P. K. 1975. Irish Adjustment to American Society: Integration or Separation? A Portrait of an Irish-Catholic Parish 1863-1886. Pittsburgh. Rec. Amer. Cath. Hist. Soc. Philadelphia. 86:7-23.

Gordan, M. 1975. The Labor Boycott in New York City, 1880-1886. Labor Hist. 16:2:184-229.

_____. 1977. Irish Immigrant Culture and the Labor Boycott in New York City, 1880-1886. In: Immigrants in Industrial America, 1850-1920. R. C. Ehrlich, ed. Univ. of Virginia, Charlottesville. pp. 111-122.

Gordon, M. A. 1977. Studies in Irish and Irish American Thought and Behavior in Guilded Age New York City. Univ. Rochester. Ph.D. dissertation.

Green, V. R. 1960. The Molly Maguire Conspiracy in the Pennsylvania Anthracite Region 1862-1879. Univ. of Rochester. Masters thesis.

Griffen, C. 1969. Workers Divided: The Effect of Craft and Ethnic Differences in Poughkeepsie, New York, 1850-1880. In: Nineteenth-Century Cities. S. Thernstrom and R. Sennett, eds. Yale Univ. Press, New Haven, 49-96.

Griffen, C. and S. Griffen. 1978. Natives and Newcomers: The Ordering of Opportunity in Poughkeepsie, New York 1850-1880. Harvard Univ., Cambridge.

Griffin, M. J. J. 1911. Religion of Early Irish Immigrants to Pennsylvania. Amer. Cath. Hist. Res. 7:170-172.

Groneman, C. 1973. The Bloody Ould Sixth: A Social Analysis of a Mid-Nineteenth Century New York City Working Class Community. Univ. of Rochester. Ph.D. dissertation.

_____. 1977. She Earns As A Child -- She Pays As A Man: Women Workers in a Mid-Nineteenth Century New York City Community. In: Immigrants in Industrial America 1850-1920, R. L. Ehrlich, ed. Univ. of Virginia, Charlottesville. pp. 33-46.

_____. 1978. Working Class Immigrant Women in Mid-Nineteenth Century New York: The Irish Woman's Experience. J. Urban History. 4:3:255-273.

Gudelunas, W. A., Jr. and W. G. Shade. 1976. Before the Molly Maguires: The Emergence of the Ethno-Religious Factor in the Politics of the Lower Anthracite Region. 1844-72. Arno Press, New York.

Hackett, J. D. 1932. Philadelphia Irish. J. Irish Amer. Hist. Soc. 30:103-117.

Harris, S. H. 1960. John Louis O'Sullivan and the Election of 1844 in New York. New York Hist. 44:278-298.

Hastings, H. 1910. Irish Stars in the Archives of New York Province. J. Amer. Irish Hist. Soc. 9:152-160.

Herlihy, E., ed. 1932. Fifty Years of Boston. Boston Tercentenary Committee, Boston.

Hindman, J. F. 1960. The Irishman Who Developed American Culture. Amer. Cath. Hist. Soc. Rec. 71:23-30.

Hinkel, J. V. 1960. St. Patricks: Mother Church of Washington. Columbia Hist. Soc. Rec. 57-59:33-43.

Itter, W. A. 1934. Early Labor Troubles in the Schuylkill Anthracite Region. Penna. Hist. 1:28-37.

_____. 1941. Conscriptions in Pennsylvania During the Civil War. Univ. of Southern California. Masters thesis.

Jones, W. D. 1967. Made in New York: A Plot to Kill the Queen. New York Hist. Soc. Quart. 51:311-325.

Judson, E. Z. C. 1848. Mysteries and Miseries of New York. Berford, New York.

Kane, J. J. 1950. The Irish Immigrant in Philadelphia, 1840-1860: A Study of Conflict and Accommodations. Univ. of Penna. Ph.D. dissertation.

_____. 1955. Philadelphia Irish. Information. 69:40-46.

Kennedy, J. H. 1930. Thomas Dongan Governor of New York 1682-1688. The Catholic University of America Studies in American Church History No. 9. Washington, D.C.

Lannie, V. P. and B. C. Diethorns. 1968. For the Honor and Glory of God: The Philadelphia Bible Riots of 1840. Hist. Educ. Quart. 8:44-106.

Laurie, B. 1971. The Working People of Philadelphia 1827-1853. Univ. of Pittsburgh. Ph.D. dissertation.

_____. et al. 1977. Immigrants and Industry. The Philadelphia Experience, 1850-1880. In: Immigrants in Industrial America 1850-1920. R. L. Ehrlich, ed. Univ. of Virginia, Charlottesville. pp. 123-150.

Lewinson, E. R. 1965. John Purroy Mitchel: The Boy Mayor of New York. Astra Books, New York.

Lewis, A. H. 1977. Those Philadelphia Kellys: With a Touch of Grace. Morrow, New York.

Light, D. B., Jr. 1979. Class, Ethnicity and the Urban Ecology in a Nineteenth Century City: Philadelphia Irish 1840-1890. Univ. Pennsylvania. Ph.D. dissertation.

Limpus, L. M. 1940. History of the New York Fire Department. Dutton, New York.

Lippard, G. 1854. New York: Its Upper Ten and Lower Million. Menderhall, Cincinnati.

London, H. 1967. The Irish and American Nativism in New York City 1843-47. Dublin Rev. 240:378-394.

Mahony, W. H. 1922. American-Irish Prominent in New Jersey State and Local Government. J. Amer. Irish Hist. Soc. 21:125-131.

_____. 1922. The Irish Element in Newark, New Jersey. J. Amer. Irish Hist. Soc. 21:131-145.

_____. 1926. The Melting Pot - Irish Footsteps in New Jersey. J. Amer. Irish Hist. Soc. 25:159-178.

_____. 1927. Some 17th Century Irish Colonists in New Jersey. J. Amer. Irish Hist. Soc. 26:242-246.

_____. 1927. Irish Footsteps in New Jersey Sands. J. Amer. Irish Hist. Soc. 26:247-254.

_____. 1928. The Irish in Princeton, New Jersey. J. Amer. Irish Hist. Soc. 27:314-320.

_____. 1930. Irish Settlers in Union County, New Jersey. J. Amer. Irish Hist. Soc. 28:83-85.

Man, A. P. 1950. The Irish in New York in the Early Eighteen-Sixties. Irish Historical Studies. 7:81-108.

Man, A. P., Jr. 1951. Labor Competition and the New York Draft Riots of 1863. J. Negro History. 36:375-405.

Maths, M. C. 1975. The Irish Family in Buffalo, New York, 1855-1875: A Sociohistorical Analysis. Washington Univ. Ph.D. dissertation.

McCaffrey, L. J. 1929-30. The Emerald Association of Brooklyn. J. Amer. Irish Hist. Soc. 28:142-147.

McCarthy, C. A. 1969. The Great Molly Maguire Hoax: Based on Information Suppressed 90 years. Cro-Woods Publ., Wyoming, Pennsylvania.

McConville, M. St. Patrick. 1928. Political Nativism in the State of Maryland, 1830-1860. Catholic Univ. Washington.

McGinley, C. 1966. Irish-American's in Philadelphia and Their Involvement with the Irish Independence Movement. Temple Univ. Paper History Dept. Seminar.

McGirr, N. F. 1949. The Irish in the Early Days of the District. Columbia Hist. Soc. Rec. 48-49: 93-96.

McGivern, E. P. 1979. Ethnic Identity and Its Relation to Group Norms: Irish-Americans in Metropolitan Pittsburgh. Univ. of Pittsburgh. Ph.D. dissertation.

McKelvey, G. 1949. Rochester the Flower City, 1855-1900. Harvard, Cambridge.

McKenna, J. J. 1951. Early Irish in Berks County (1709-1944). Hist. Rev. Berks Co. 17:20-21, 25, 27, 29.

McKenrick, C. R. 1940. New Munster. Maryland Hist. Magz. 35:147-159.

McManus, T. J. 1924. A Few Outstanding Figures of Irish Ancestry at the Bench and Bar of New York. J. Amer. Irish Hist. Soc. 23:101-114.

Meehan, T. F. 1904. Pioneer Times in Brooklyn. U.S. Cath. Hist. Soc., Hist. Rec. and Stud. 3:115-130.

_____. 1913. New Yorks First Irish Emigrant Society. U.S. Cath. Hist. Rec. 6:pt 2:202-211.

_____. 1940. A Dutch Irish Pact, 1680. United States Cath. Hist. Soc. Hist. Rec. and Stud. 31:152-156.

_____. 1946. A Dutch Irish Pact, 1680. U.S. Cath. Hist. Soc. Rev. 31:152-156.

Meyers, A. C. 1902. Immigration of the Irish Quakers into Pennsylvania, 1682-1750, With Their Early History in Ireland. Published by A. C. Myers. Swarthmore, Pennsylvania.

Miller, D. T. 1968. Immigration and Social Stratification in Pre-Civil War New York, New York. Hist. 49:157-168.

Mitchell, A. G., Jr. 1976. Irish Family Patterns in 19th Century Ireland and Lowell, Massachusetts. Boston Univ. Ph.D. dissertation.

Monahan, K. 1977. The Irish Hour: An Expression of Musical Taste and the Cultural Value of the Pittsburg Irish Community. Ethnicity. 4:1:201-215.

Morgan, G. 1926. Philadelphia City of Firsts. Hist. Publ. Soc., Philadelphia.

Moynihan, D. P. 1961. When the Irish Ran New York. Reporter. 24:32-34.

_____. 1963. The Irish. In: Beyond the Melting Pot. D. P. Moynihan and N. Glazer. M.I.T. Press, Cambridge, Massachusetts. pp. 271-291.

_____. 1963. Irish of New York. Commentary. 36:93-107.

Muirhead, J. F. 1960. Thomas Addis Emmet (1764-1841). New Eng. J. Med. 262:460-61.

Mulvey, H. F., ed. 1953. Richard O'Gorman New York City in 1859: A Letter to William Smith New York State Hist. 34:85-96.

Murphy, R. C. and L. Mannion. 1962. The History of the Society of the Friendly Sons of St. Patrick in the City of New York. 1784-1955. Murphy and Mannion, New York.

Myers, A. C. 1902. The Immigration of the Irish Quakers into Pennsylvania 1682-1750. A. C. Myers, Swarthmore, Pennsylvania (reprinted Geneological Publ. Co.).

Nelson, W. 1912. The Discovery and Early History of New Jersey: A Paper Read Before the Passiac County Historical Society, June 11, 1872.

New Jersey Cath. Hist. Rec. Comm. 1978. The Bishops of Newark 1853-1973. Seton Hall Univ. Press, South Orange, New Jersey.

Nolan, J. B. 1954. The Battle of Womelsdorf. Penna. Magz. Hist. Biog. 78:361-368.

Northampton County Hist. and Geneological Society. 1926. The Scotch-Irish of Northampton County, Pennsylvania. J. S. Correll, Easton, Pennsylvania.

O'Brien, M. J. 1906. Irish Settlers in Pennsylvania. J. Amer. Irish Hist. Soc. 6:37-45.

_____. 1907. Irish Colonists in New York. Proc. New York St. Hist. Assn. 7:94-123.

_____. 1914. Early Pittsburgh, Pennsylvania. J. Amer. Irish Hist. Soc. 13:205-208.

_____. 1914. Some Interesting Notes on Washington, D.C. J. Amer. Irish Hist. Soc. 13:227-229.

_____. 1916. Irish Property Owners and Businessmen of New York City in the Seventeenth and Eighteenth Centuries. J. Amer. Irish Hist. Soc. 15:243-277.

_____. 1918. The Irish Burghers of New Amsterdam and Freemen of New York. J. Amer. Irish Hist. Soc. 17:146-148.

_____. 1919. Irish Pioneers in Delaware. J. Amer. Irish Hist. Soc. 18:187-197.

_____. 1919. Irish Pioneers and Schoolmasters in Butler County, Pennsylvania. J. Amer. Irish Hist. Soc. 18:198-204.

_____. 1922. The Cumberland County, Pennsylvania Militia in the Revolution. J. Amer. Irish Hist. Soc. 21:121-124.

_____. 1922. The First Regiment of the Pennsylvania Line. J. Amer. Irish Hist. Soc. 21:111-117.

_____. 1922. The Kellys, Burkes and Sheas of Massachusetts Line. J. Amer. Irish Hist. Soc. 21:107-110.

_____. 1925. The Irish in Montgomery and Washington Counties, Maryland in 1778. J. Amer. Irish Hist. Soc. 24:157-161.

_____. 1927. New Munster, New Ireland County, Maryland. J. Amer. Irish Hist. Soc. 26:30-44.

_____. 1927. Some First Families of Virginia. J. Amer. Irish Hist. Soc. 26:70-83.

_____. 1927. The Irish and the Dutch in Albany, New York, Colonial Records. J. Amer. Irish Hist. Soc. 26:105-118.

_____. 1927. The Irish in New London, Connecticut in the 17th and 18th Centuries. The Interesting Diary of Joshua Hempstead. J. Amer. Irish Hist. Soc. 26:182-191.

_____. 1927. The Irish in the Dutch Records of Ulster County, New York. Amer. Irish Hist. J. 26: 129-136.

_____. 1927. The Pioneer Irish of Essex County, Massachusetts. J. Amer. Irish Hist. Soc. 26:137-149.

_____. 1928. In Old New York. The Irish Dead in Trinity and St. Paul's Churchyards. Amer. Irish Hist. Soc. New York.

_____. 1928. Irish Pioneers in Berks County, Pennsylvania. J. Amer. Irish Hist. Soc. 27:39-45.

_____. 1928. Irish Pioneers in Hartford County, Connecticut. J. Amer. Irish Hist. Soc. 27:200-228.

_____. 1928. Irish Settlers in Queens County in New York. J. Amer. Irish Hist. Soc. 27:101-113.

_____. 1928. Irish Settlers in Orange County, New York. J. Amer. Irish Hist. Soc. 27:114-123.

_____. 1928. The Irish in New Jersey Probate Records. J. Amer. Irish Hist. Soc. 27:76-100.

Pessen, E. 1971. Did Fortunes Rise and Fall Mecurial in Antebellum America? The Tale of Two Cities: Bosto and New York. J. Soc. Hist. 4:339-357.

Purcell, R. J. 1928. The Irish Contribution to Colonial New York. Studies. 27:41-60.

_____. 1934. Education and Irish Schoolmasters in Maryland's National Period. Cath. Educ. Rev. 32:198-207.

_____. 1934. Irish Colonists in Colonial Maryland. Studies: An Irish Quart. Rev. 23:279-294.

_____. 1935. Immigration from the Canal Era to the Civil War. History of the State of New York. V 7, 31-59. In: History of New York State. A. C. Flick, ed. Columbia Univ., New York.

_____. 1937. Irish Cultural Contribution in Early New York. Cath. Ed. Rev. 25:449-460.

_____. 1938. Irish Cultural Contribution in Early New York. Cath. Ed. Rev. 26:28-42.

_____. 1938. The Irish Emigrant Society of New York. Studies: An Irish Quart. Rev. 27:583-599.

_____. 1939. Irish Educational Contribution to Colonial Pennsylvania. Cath. Educ. Rev. 37:425-439.

_____. 1940. Irish Contribution to Colonial New York. Studies: An Irish Quart. Rev. 29:591-607.

_____. 1940. Irish Educational Contribution to Pennsylvania in the National Period. Cath. Educ. Rev. 38:467-480, 537-549.

_____. 1947. Irish Settlers in the Delaware Valley. Pa. Hist. 14:94-107.

_____. 1948. The New York Commissioners of Emigration and Irish Immigrants 1847-1860. Studies: An Irish Quart. Rev. 37:29-42.

_____. 1960. Irish Settlers in Early New Jersey: Colony and State. New Jersey Genesis, 6:222,224-227, 236-239, 248-250.

Quillen, I. J. 1932. A History of the Five Points to 1890. Yale Univ. Masters thesis.

Reilly, D. 1949. An Irish-American Chemist, William James MacNeven, 1763-1841. Chymia. 2:17-26.

Rhodes, J. F. 1910. The Molly Maguires in the Anthracite Region of Pennsylvania. Amer. Hist. Rev. 15:3:547-561.

Rodechko, J. 1973. Irish-American Society in the Pennsylvania Anthracite Region 1870-1880. In: The Ethnic Experience in Philadelphia. J. E. Bodner, ed. Bucknell Univ., Lewisberg, Pennsylvania. pp. 19-38.

Rowley, W. E. 1968. Albany, A Tale of Two Cities 1820-1880. Harvard Univ. Ph.D. dissertation.

_____. 1971. The Irish Aristocracy of Albany, 1798-1878. New York Hist. 52:275-304.

Runcie, J. 1972. Hunting the Nigs in Philadelphia: The Race Riot of 1834. Penna. Hist. 39:187-218.

Saint Henry, M. 1936. Nativism in Pennsylvania With Particular Regard to Its Effect on Politics and Education, 1840-1860. Rec. Amer. Cath. Hist. Soc., Philadelphia. 67:5-47.

Schlegel, M. W. 1943. The Workingman's Benevolent Association: First Union of Anthracite Miners. Penna. Hist. 10:243-267.

Scisco, L. D. 1901. Political Nativism in New York State. Columbia Univ., New York.

Scully, D. J. 1907. Irish Influence in the Life of Baltimore. J. Amer. Irish Hist. Soc. 7:69-75.

Shaw, D. V. 1972. The Making of an Immigrant City: Ethnic and Cultural Conflict in Jersey City, New Jersey, 1850-1877. Univ. of Rochester. Ph.D. dissertation. (reprinted 1976, Arno Press, New York)

_____. 1977. Political Leadership in the Industrial City. Irish Development and Nativist Response in Jersey City. In: Immigrants in Industrial Americ 1850-1920. R. L. Ehrlich, ed. Univ. of Virginia, Charlottesville. pp. 85-95.

Sheppard, J. H. 1925. Irish Preachers and Educators in the Early History of the Presbyterian Church in Ireland. J. Amer. Irish Hist. Soc. 24:162-174.

Sheridan, P. B. 1957. The Immigrants in Philadelphia. 1827-1860: The Contemporary Published Report.
Georgetown Univ. Ph.D. dissertation.

Smith, N. J. 1971. Footloose and Fancy Free: The
Demography and Sociology of a Runaway Class in
Colonial Pennsylvania, 1771-1776. Bryn Mawr.
Masters paper.

Spotts, C. D. 1960. The Gault Graveyard, Lancaster
County. Hist. Soc. J. 64:34-48.

Stewart, J. 1897. Obstructions to Irish Immigration
to Pennsylvania 1736. Penna. Magz. Hist. Biog.
21:485-87.

Sullivan. W. A. 1948. Philadelphia Labor. During
the Jackson Era. Penna. Hist. 15:1-16.

_____. 1954. The Industrial Revolution and the
Factory Operatives in Penna. Panna. Magz. Hist. and
Biog. 78:476-477.

_____. 1955. The Industrial Worker in Pennsyl-
vania 1800-1840. Pa. Historical and Museum Commission,
Harrisburg.

Tully, J. J., Jr. 1976. Irish Pioneers in Northern
New York. The Recorder. 37:127-140.

Tuska, B. 1925. Know Nothingism in Baltimore, 1854-
1860. Cath. Hist. Rev. 11:217-251.

Vinyard, J. M. 1975. On the Fringe in Philadelphia.
J. Urban Hist. 1:4:492-498.

Ward, S. D. 1937. New York City in 1842. New York
Hist. Soc. Quart. 21:4.

Walker, S. 1978. The Police and the Community
Scranton, Pennsylvania, 1866-1884. American Studies.
6:1:79-90.

Weinbaum, P. O. 1975. Temperance, Politics and the
New York City Riots of 1857. New York Hist. Soc.
Quart. 59:3:246-270.

White, P. L. 1967. An Irish Immigrant Housewife on the New York Frontier. New York Hist. 48:182-188.

Williams, H. A. 1957. History of the Hibernian Society of Baltimore, 1803-1957. Hibernian Soc. of Baltimore, Baltimore.

Chapter 13: THE IRISH IN THE NORTH CENTRAL STATES

Anderson, M. J. 1934. Autobiography. Minneapolis.

_____. 1967. From an Irish Farm to a Minnesota Homestead. Gopher Historian. 21:21-26.

Bower, W. 1966. A Glimpse Into a City's Past. Ann. of Iowa. 38:5:363-87.

Bradley, D. S. and M. N. Zald. 1965. From Commercial Elite to Political Administrator: The Recruitment of Mayors of Chicago. Amer. J. Socio. 71:153-167.

Browne, H. J. 1950. Archbishop Hughes and Western Colonization. Cath. Hist. Rev. 36:257-285.

Butler, T. A. 1874. The Irish on the Prairie. D. and J. Sadlier & Company, New York, Montreal.

Calkin, H. L. 1964. The Irish in Iowa. Palimpset. 45:33-96.

Callahan, N. J. and W. F. Hickey. 1978. Irish Americans and Their Communities of Cleveland. Cleveland State Univ., Cleveland.

Campbell, B. C. 1975-76. Ethnicity and the 1893 Wisconsin Assembly. J. Amer. Hist. 62:74-94.

Carroon, R. G. 1971. John Gregory and the Irish Immigration to Milwaukee. Historical Messenger for the Milwaukee County Historical Society. 27:51-64.

Cashman, W., ed. 1976. Journal of Beaver Island History, VI. Beaver Island Hist. Society, St. James, Michigan.

Casper, H. W. 1966. History of the Church in Nebrasks. V. 3, Catholic Chapter in Nebraska Immigration. Bruce, Milwaukee.

Coad, R. G. 1936. Irish Pioneers of Nebraska.
Nebr. Hist. Magz. 17:171-177.

Cochran, A. L. 1958. The Saga of an Irish Immigrant Family: The Descendants of John Mullanphy.
St. Louis Univ. Ph.D. dissertation. (reprinted
1976, Arno Press, New York).

Collar, H. 1976. Irish Migration to Beaver Island.
In: The Journal of Beaver Island History. VI.
Beaver Island Historical Society, St. James, Michigan.
pp. 27-50.

Colton, K. E. 1940. Parnell's Mission to Iowa.
Annals of Iowa: A Hist. Quart. 22:312-321.

Conzen, K. N. 1976. Immigrant Milwaukee 1836-1860.
Harvard Univ. Press, Cambridge.

Cook, F. F. 1910. Bygone Days in Chicago: Recollections of the "Garden City" of the Sixties.
McCling, Chicago.

Cross, R. E. et al., eds. 1968. St. Patrick, Irish-
town 1868-1964. Mt. St. Joseph Parish, St. Louis,
Michigan.

Dannenbaum, J. 1978. Immigrants and Temperance
Ethnocultural Conflicts in Cincinnati, 1845-1900.
Ohio Hist. 87:2:125-139.

Decker, D. D. n.d. The Irish Wilderness. Fay
Publ. Co. Springfield, Missouri.

Denny, J. 1977. Cultural Resource Potential of the
Irish Wilderness. Dept. Natural Resources. Jefferson
City, Missouri.

Desmond, H. J. 1930. Early Irish Settlers in Milwaukee. J. Amer. Irish Hist. Soc. 29:103-111.

_____. 1930. Early Irish Settlers in Milwaukee. Wisconsin Magz. Hist. 13:365-374.

Dondore, D. A. 1926. The Prairie and the Making of Middle America: Four Centuries of Description. The Torch Press, Cedar Rapids, Iowa.

Driscoll, C. B. 1943. Kansas Irish. Macmillan, New York.

Egan, H. E. 1925. A History of Irish Immigration to Minnesota, 1865-1890. MS. on file. Minn. Hist. Soc.

_____. 1930. Irish Immigration to Minnesota. Mid-America, 1865-1900. 12:133-166.

French, D., ed. 1897. Biographical History of the American Irish in Chicago. Amer. Biographical Printing Co., Chicago.

Funchion, M. F. 1973. Chicago's Irish Nationalists, 1881-1890. Loyola Univ., Chicago. Ph.D. dissertation. (report, 1976, Arno).

_____. 1975. Irish Nationalists and Chicago's Politics in the 1880's. Eire. 10:2:3-18.

Galford, J. B. 1957. The Foreign Born and Urban Growth in the Great Lakes 1850-1950: A Study of Chicago, Cleveland, Detroit, and Milwaukee. New York Univ., New York. Ph.D. dissertation.

Gallagher, H. S. 1930. Beaver Island, Michigan: An Irish Island Colony. J. Amer. Irish Hist. Soc. 28:198-203.

Giaquinta, J. and B. Peterson. 1978. Manuscript Collections: The Irish Preston Papers 1832-1872. Ann. Iowa. 44:6:475-479.

Gosnell, H. F. 1937. Machine Politics: Chicago Model. Univ. of Chicago. Chicago.

Hanratty, M. F. 1933. A Study of Early Irish Contributions to the Growth of St. Louis. St. Louis
Univ. Masters thesis.

Hart, T. 1976. The Religions of Beaver Island.
In: J. Beaver Island Hist. VI. Beaver Island
Hist. Soc. St. James, Michigan. pp. 103-122.

Holi, G. and P. Jones. 1977. The Ethnic Frontier:
Essays in the History of Group Survival in Chicago
and Midwest. William and Erdmans, Grand Rapids,
Michigan.

Ireland, J. 1879. Catholic Colonization in Minnesota. Catholic Colonization Bureau of Minnesota.
St. Paul.

Janis, R. 1972. The Churches of Detroit: A Study
in Urban Social Structure 1880-1940. Univ. of
Michigan. Ph.D. dissertation.

_____. 1979. Ethnic Mixture and the Persistence
of Cultural Pluralism in the Church Communities of
Detroit, 1880-1940. Mid-America. 61:2:99-115.

Lang, E. 1954. Irishman in Northern Indiana Before
1850. Mid-America. 36:190-198.

Leonard, H. B. 1976. Ethnic Conflict and Episcopal
Power. The Diocese of Cleveland 1847-1870. Cath.
Hist. Rev. 62:388-407.

Leonard, S. J. 1977. The Irish, English and Germans
in Denver 1860-1890. Colo. Magz. 54:2:126-153.

Love, G. G. 1952. I Never Thought We'd Make It.
Harcourt Brace, New York.

Lubell, S. 1952. The Chicago Irish. In: The
Future of American Politics. S. Lubell. Harper,
New York.

Luebke, F. C. 1977. Ethnic Group Settlement on the
Great Plains. West. Hist. Quart. 8:405-430.

Marling, J. M. 1955. A Pioneer Priest of Western Missouri. Ann. Eccles. Rev. 133:361-369.

Martin, M. A. 1932. Irish Catholic Colonization in the Diocese of Omaha, 1856-1890. Univ. Notre Dame. Masters thesis.

McCullough, L. E. 1978. Irish Music in Chicago: An Ethnomusicological Study. Univ. Pittsburgh. Ph.D. dissertation.

McDonald, J. 1954. History of the Irish in Wisconsin in the 19th Century. Catholic Univ., Washington, D.C.

McDonald, M. J. 1949. Irish Immigration Into Wisconsin, 1840-1860. Catholic Univ. Masters thesis.

_____. 1956-57. The Irish of the North Country. Wisc. Magz. Hist. 40:126-132.

McGoorty, J. P. 1927. Early Irish of Illinois. Ill. Hist. St. Soc. Transactions. 34:54-64.

_____. 1927. The Early Irish of Illinois. Ill. Cath. Hist. Rev. 10:26-37.

McHugh, G. H. 1939. Political Nativism in St. Louis, 1840-57. St. Louis University. Masters thesis.

Meyer, K. 1972. The Politics of Loyalty From La Follette to McCarthy in Wisconsin, 1918-1952. Univ. of Wisconsin. Ph.D. dissertation.

Mitchell, F. D. 1968. Embattled Democracy: Missouri Democratic Politics, 1919-1932. Univ. of Missouri- Columbia.

Musselman, B. L. 1976. Working Class Unity and Ethnic Division: Cincinnati Trade Unionists and Cultural Pluralism. Cincinnati Hist. Soc. Bull. 34:1:121-143.

Nelli, H. S. 1970. John Powers and the Italians: Politics in a Chicago Ward, 1896-1921. J. Amer. Hist. 57:67-84.

O'Donnell, J. H. 1939. The Catholic Church in Northern Indiana, 1830-1857. Cath. Hist. Rev. 25:135-145.

O'Dwyer, G. C. 1920. Irish Colonization in Illinois. Ill. Cath. Hist. Rev. 3:73-76.

O'Leary, C. F. 1910. The Irish in the Early Days of St. Louis. J. Amer. Irish Hist. Soc. 9:206-213.

Onahan, W. J. 1881. Irish Settlements in Illinois. The Catholic World. 33:157-162.

_____. 1917. A Chapter of Catholic Colonization. Acta et Dieta. 6:35-53.

O'Neill, J. 1876. O'Neills Irish American Colonies in Nebrasks.

Pap, M. 1973. The Irish Community of Cleveland. In: M. Pap, Ethnic Communities of Cleveland: A Reference Work. John Carroll Univ., Cleveland. pp. 179-186.

Pare, B. 1951. The Catholic Church in Detroit 1701-1888. Gabriel Richard Press, Detroit.

Pierce, B. L. 1937, 1940, 1957. A History of Chicago, 3 Volumes. Univ. of Chicago, Chicago.

Piggott, M. 1910. Irish Pioneers of the Upper Mississippi Valley. J. Amer. Irish Hist. Soc. 9:301-330.

Piper, R. M. n.d. The Irish in Chicago. Univ. of Chicago. Masters thesis.

Qualey, C. C. 1950. Some National Groups in Minnesota. Minnesota History. 31:18-32.

Read, M. J. 1941. A Population Study of the Drift-less Hill Land During the Pioneer Period, 1832-1860. Univ. of Wisconsin. Ph.D. dissertation.

Reddig, W. 1947. Tom's Town: Kansas City and the Pendergast Legend. Lippincott, New York.

Robinson, D., ed. 1912. Fenians in Dakota. South Dakota Hist. Soc. 6:117-130b.

Rogers, V. A. 1972. The Irish in Cincinnati, 1860-1870: A Typical Experience. Univ. of Cincinnati. Masters thesis.

Scanlan, C. M. 1914. History of the Irish in Wisconsin. J. Irish Amer. Hist. Soc. 13:237-260.

Schafer, J. 1952. Know-Nothingism in Wisconsin. Wisc. Magz. Hist. 8:3-21.

Senning, J. P. 1914-15. The Know Nothing Movement in Illinois. J. Ill. St. Hist. Soc. 7:9-29.

Shannon, J. F. 1957. Bishop Irelands Connemara Experiment. Minn. Hist. 35:205-213.

_____. 1957. Catholic Colonization on the Frontier. Yale Univ., New Haven.

Sirjamaki, J. 1946. The People of the Mesabi Range. Minn. Hist.. 27:203-215.

Smith, A. E. 1928. The Sweetman Irish Colony. Minnesota History. 9:331-346.

Smith, M. S. 1958. The Influence of the Irish Vote in Chicago and the Elections of 1884, 1888 and 1892. Univ. of Notre Dame. Masters thesis.

Sullivan, J. B. 1926. Kate Shelley, An Irish Heroine of Iowa. J. Amer. Irish Hist. Soc. 25:195-201.

Sullivan, M. L. 1971. Fighting for Irish Freedom: St. Louis Irish-Americans, 1918-1922. Missouri Hist. Rev. 65:184-206.

_____. 1972. Constitutionalism Revolution and Culture, Irish-American Nationalism in St. Louis, 1902-1914. Mo. Hist. Soc. Bull. 28:4:234-245.

_____. 1976. Where Did all the Irish Go? The Irish in St. Louis 1900-1925. Organiz. Amer. Historian 69th Ann. Mtg. St. Louis, April 7-10, 1976.

_____. 1977. St. Louis Ethnic Neighborhoods. 1850-1930. Mo. Hist. Soc. Bull. 33:64-76.

Sweetman, J. 1885. Farms for Sale in the Sweetman Catholic Colony of Murry County Minnesota. Irish-American Colonization Co., St. Paul.

_____. 1911. The Sweetman Catholic Colony of Currie, Minnesota: A Memoir. Acta et Dicta. 3:41-61.

Tarr, J. A. 1966. J. R. Walsh of Chicago: A Case Study in Banking and Politics 1881-1905. Bus. Hist. Rev. 40:451-466.

Thompson, J. J. 1919. Irish Settlers in Early Illinois. Illinois Cath. Hist. Rev. 2:223-238.

_____. 1920. The Irish in Chicago. Ill. Cath. Hist. Rev. 2:458-473.

_____. 1920. The Irish in Chicago. Ill. Cath. Hist. Rev. 3:146-169.

_____. 1920. The Irish in Early Illinois. Ill. Cath. Hist. Rev. 3:286-302.

Titus, W. A. 1925. Meeme: A Frontier Settlement That Developed Strong Men. Wisc. Magz. Hist. 4:281-286.

VanDoren, R. F. 1965. Myth-History of the Irish Wilderness. Shannon County Historical Review. July, 1965. No. 6.

Vinyard, J. E. 1974. Inland Urban Immigrants. The Detroit Irish 1850. Michigan History. 57:121-139.

Vinyard, J. N. 1972. The Irish on the Urban Frontier: Detroit 1850-1880. Univ. of Michigan. Ph.D. dissertation (reprinted 1976, Arno Press, New York).

Vogler, I. 1976. The Roman Catholic Culture Region of Central Minnesota. Pioneer America, Falls Church, Virginia. 8:2:71-83.

Wallace, E. M. 1925. Early Farmers in Exeter. Wisc. Magz. Hist. 7:415-422.

Ward, F. J. 1906. Early Irish in St. Louis, Missouri. J. Amer. Irish Hist. Soc. 5:46-50.

Watson, R. A. 1964. Religion and Politics in Mid-America: Presidential Voting in Missouri 1928 and 1960. Midcontinental Amer. Stud. J. 5:33-55.

Wendt, L. and H. Kogan. 1967. Bosses in Lusty Chicago. Indiana Univ., Bloomington, Indiana.

Whelan, L. F. 1940. 'Them's They' The Story of Monches, Wisconsin. Wisc. Magz. Hist. 24:39-55.

Whyte, W. F. 1921. Chronicle of Early Watertown, Wisc. Magz. Hist. 4:287-314.

Wihebrink, R. 1974. History of the Irish Wilderness Country. USDA - Forest Service Mark Twain National Forest.

Chapter 14: THE IRISH IN THE SOUTH AND SOUTHWEST

Anon. 1902. Galway Catholics as Settlers on Land of Washington. Amer. Cath. Hist. Res. 19:128-131.

_____. 1914. Extracts from the Will Books of Spotsylvania County. J. Amer. Irish Hist. Soc. 13:225-227.

Biddle, S. F. 1947. Hibernia, The Unreturning Tide. Biddle, New York.

Carroll, K. L. 1976. The Irish Quaker Community at Camden, South Carolina. Hist. Magz. 77:2:69-83.

Chalker, F. 1970. Irish Catholics in the Building of the Ocmulgee and Flint Railroad. Ga. Hist. Quart. 54:507-516.

Clayton, L. W. 1977. The Irish Peddler Boy and Old Deery Inn. Tenn. Hist. Quart. 36:2:149-160.

Cobb, I. S. 1919. The Lost Irish Tribes in the South. Friends of Irish Freedom, Washington.

_____. 1931. The Lost Irish Tribes in the South. Tenn. Hist. Magz. 2nd series. 1:115-124.

Conway, A. 1962. New Orleans as a Port of Immigration. Louisiana Studies. I:1-22.

Cosgrove, J. I. 1926. Hibernian Society of Charleston, South Carolina. J. Amer. Hist. Soc. 25:150-158.

Din, G. C. 1971. The Irish Mission to West Florida. Louisiana Hist. 12:315-334.

Doyle, J. E. 1974. Chicopee's Irish 1830-1875. Hist. J. West. Mass. 3:13-23.

Dufour, C. L., ed. 1958. St. Patricks of New Orleans. New Orleans.

Evans, J. B. 1931. Irish Priests in Early Florida. J. Amer. Irish Hist. Soc. 32:74-78.

Gilmore, H. W. 1944. The Old New Orleans and the New: A Case for Ecology. Amer. Socio. Rev. 9:385-394.

Gordon, D. 1957. The first "Western" Author. New Mexico Magz. 35:7:25-27, 66.

Greer, G. C. 1914. Early Immigrants to Virginia (1623 to 1666). J. Amer. Irish Hist. Soc. 13:209-213.

Hannon, W. B. 1911. Irish Builders of North Carolina J. Amer. Irish Hist. Soc. 10:258-261.

Harper, J. V. 1977. The Irish Travellers of Georgia. Univ. of Georgia. Ph.D. dissertation.

Kennedy, P. W. 1964. The Know-Nothing Movement in Kentucky: Role of M. J. Spalding, Catholic Bishop of Louisville. Filson Club Hist. Quart. 38:20-30.

Kenny, M. 1933. The Irish in "the South." Studies: An Irish Quart. Rev. 22:89-100.

Kenrick, C. R. 1940. Story of New Munster, Maryland. Maryland Hist. Magz. 35:147-159.

Koester, L. 1948. Louisvilles "Bloody Monday" - August 6, 1855. Hist. Bull. 26:53-54, 62-64.

McGann, A. G. 1944. Nativism in Kentucky, 1860. Catholic Univ., Washington, D.C.

McGinty, G. W. and E. Conly. 1976. Cullen Thomas Conly: American Irish Stowaway 1820-1876. Rushing, Shreveport, Louisiana.

Mese, W. A. 1922. Colonel John Montgomery, An "Irishman full of fight" Commander-in-Chief of the Virginia Troops in the County of Illinois. Ill. Cath. Hist. Rev. 5:51-58.

Monaghan, F. 1934. The Proposed Settlement of New Ireland in Kentucky. Miss. Valley Hist. Rev. 20:399-402.

Murphy, W. S. 1960. Irish Brigade of Spain and the Capture of Penasacola, 1781. Fla. Hist. Quart. 38:3: 216-225.

Neu, I. 1967. From Kilkenny to Louisiana: Notes on Eighteenth-Century Irish Emigration. Mid-America. 49:101-114.

Neville, G. K. 1973. Kinfolks and the Covenant: Ethnic Community Among Southern Presbyterians. Proc. Amer. Ethnol. Soc. 258-274.

Nichaus, E. F. 1905. Irish in New Orleans, 1800-1860. Louisiana St., Baton Rouge, Louisiana.

_____. 1961. The Irish in New Orleans 1803-1862. Tulane Univ. Ph.D. dissertation.

Oberste, W. H. 1953. Texas Irish Empresarios and their Colonies. Von Boeckmann-Jones, Austin, Texas.

O'Brien, M. J. 1907. A Glance at Some Pioneer Irish in the South. J. Amer. Irish Hist. Soc. 7:45-58.

_____. 1914. Extracts from Virginia Marriage Records. J. Amer. Irish Hist. Soc. 13:219-224.

_____. 1914. Grantees of Land in the Colony and State of Virginia. J. Amer. Irish Hist. Soc. 13:214-219.

_____. 1916. Irish Pioneers in Kentucky. By the Author, New York.

_____. 1919. Extracts from Virginia Church Records. J. Amer. Irish Hist. Soc. 18:205-207.

_____. 1921. Extracts from Virginia Records. J. Amer. Irish Hist. Soc. 18:205-207.

_____. 1922. Major Patrick Carr and Captain Patrick McGriff, Two Tallant Officers of the Georgia Continental Law. J. Amer. Irish Hist. Soc. 21:193-196.

_____. 1922. Patrick McCann Hero of the Border.
J. Amer. Irish Hist. Soc. 21:79-85.

_____. 1922. The Murphys in Virginia: Patrick
Murphy a Brave Soldier of the Virginia Continental
Line. J. Amer. Irish Hist. Soc. 21:103-106.

_____. 1925. Land Grants to Irish Settlers in
the Colony and State of Virginia. J. Amer. Irish
Hist. Soc. 24:87-124.

_____. 1926. Land Bounty Certificates of Virginia
J. Amer. Irish Hist. Soc. 25:105-109.

_____. 1926. Obituary Notices in Providence
Rhode Island Newspapers. J. Amer. Irish Hist. Soc.
25:116-124.

_____. 1926. Pioneer Irish Families in Virginia.
The Meades and Sullivans. J. Amer. Irish Hist. Soc.
25:90-104.

_____. 1926. The Irish in Charleston, South
Carolina. J. Amer. Irish Hist. Soc. 25:134-146.

_____. 1926. The Virginia Regiment - Commanded
by Colonel George Washington. J. Amer. Irish Hist.
Soc. 25:110-115.

_____. 1928. Items Cullef from the National
Gazette and Literary Register. J. Amer. Irish Hist.
Soc. 27:184-189.

_____. 1928. Pioneer Irish Settlers in Rockingham
County, Virginia. J. Amer. Irish Hist. Soc. 27:46-54

O'Connell, J. J. 1879. Catholicity in the Carolinas
and Georgia, 1820-1857. Sadlier, New York.

O'Grady, J. P. 1969. Anthony M. Keiley (1832-1905):
Virginia's Catholic Politician. Cath. Hist. Rev.
54:4:613-635.

_____. 1972. Immigrants and the Politics of
Reconstruction in Richmond, Virginia Records. Amer.
Cath. Hist. Soc., Philadelphia. 83:87-101.

O'Neal, W. B. 1960. Primitive Into Painter: Life and Letters of John Toole, 1815-1860. Univ. Virginia, Charlottesville, Virginia.

Ousley, S. 1979. The Kentucky Irish American. Filson Club Hist. Quart. 53:2:178-195.

Owen, P. 1978. Is It True What They Say About the Irish. West. Tenn. Hist. Soc. Papers. 32:120-132.

Page, D. P. 1966. Bishop Michael J. Curley and Anti Catholic Nativism in Florida. Fla. Hist. Quart. 45: 2:101-117.

Reville, J. 1937. 560 Irish Immigrants Who Came to South Carolina, 1768. Columbia, South Carolina.

Rice, B. 1932. The Irish in Texas. J. Amer. Irish Hist. Soc. 30:60-70.

Shugg, R. 1936. Suffrage and Representation in Antibellum Louisiana, Louisiana Hist. Quart. 19:396-397.

Shute, J. R. 1932. The Irish in North Carolina. J. Royal Soc. of Antiquaries of Ireland. 62:116-119.

Stanton, W. B. 1952. The Irish of Memphis (since 1819). West Tenn. Hist. Soc. Papers. 6:87-118.

Stritch, T. J. 1978. Three Catholic Bishops From Tennessee. Tenn. Hist. Quart. 37:1:3-35.

Sweeney, W. M. 1924. Some Pioneer Irishman of Virginia and North Carolina. Recorder. 2:9-11.

Sweeny, W. N. and L. H. Sweeny. 1932. Virginia County Records of the 17th and 18th Centuries. Amer. Irish Hist. Soc. 30:122-133.

Tanner, H. H. 1963. Zespedes in East Florida. Univ. Miami Hispanic Amer. Studies, No. 19. Coral Gables, Univ. of Miani Press.

Tobin, W. A. n.d. The Irish in South Carolina. Florence, South Carolina.

Toker, F.  1970.  James O'Donnell:  An Irish Georgian in America.  J. Soc. Arch. Hist. 29:132-143.

Weaver, H.  1953.  Foreigners in Antibellum Savanna, Georgia Hist. Quart. 37:1-17.

Williams, V. F.  1923.  McCullough and His Irish Settlement.  North Carolina Booklet.  22:32-39.

Chapter 15:   THE IRISH IN THE FARWEST

Barry, B.  1969.  From Shamrocks to Sagebrush.
Examiner Publ. Co., Lakeview, Oregon.

Blessing, P. J.  1977.  West Among Strangers:  Irish
Migration to California 1850-1880.  Univ. of California.  Ph.D. dissertation.

Breatnac, S.  1978.  The Difference Remains.  In:
The Irish in San Francisco.  J. P. Walsh, ed.  Irish
Literary Historical Soc., San Francisco.  pp. 143-150.

Brusher, J. S.  1951.  Peter Yorke and the A.P.A. in
San Francisco.  The Catholic Historical Rev. 37:129-
150.

Bullough, W. A.  1978.  Chris Buckley and San Francisco:
The Man and the City.  In:  The Irish in San Francisco.
J. P. Walsh, ed.  Irish Liter. Hist. Soc. San Francisco.
pp. 27-41.

Burchell, R. A.  1971.  British Immigrants in Southern
California, 1850-1870.  S. California Quart. 53:283-301.

_____.  1978.  San Francisco Irish.  Current Anthro-
pology. 19:2:458.

_____.  1980.  The San Francisco Irish 1848-1880.
Univ. California, Berkeley.

Callow, A. B.  1956.  San Francisco's Blind Boss.
Pacific Hist. Rev. 25:261-279.

Camp. C. L., ed.  1928.  An Irishman in the Gold Rush:
The Journal of Thomas Kerr.  California Historical
Society Quarterly. 7:3:205-227; 7:4:395-404.

_____.  1929.  An Irishman in the Gold Rush:  The
Journal of Thomas Kerr.  California Historical Society
Quarterly. 8:1:17-25; 8:2:167-182; 8:3:262-277.

Cronin, B. C.  1943.  Father Yorke and the Labor
Movement in San Francisco, 1900-1910.  Catholic Univ.,
Washington.

Crowley, G. T. 1936. The Irish in California Studies: An Irish Quart. Rev. 25:451-462.

Dancis, B. 1978. Social Mobility and Class Consciousness: San Francisco International Workers Association in the 1880's. J. Soc. Hist. 11:75-98.

Digby, M. 1949. Horace Plunkett: An Anglo-American Irishman. Blackwell, Oxford.

Dwyer, Bishop R. J. 1957. The Irish in the Building of the Inter-Mountain West. Irish Eccles. Rev. 87:401-419.

Enright, J. S. 1954. Catholic Pioneer in Donner Party. Acad. Scrapbook. 4:193-203.

Erie, S. P. 1975. The Development of Class and Ethnic Politics in San Francisco 1870-1910: A Critique of the Pluralist Interpretation. Univ. California. Ph.D. dissertation.

_____. 1978. Politics and Public Sector and Irish Social Mobility, San Francisco 1870-1900. West Polit. Quart. 31:2:274-289.

Gallagher, H. S. 1932. "Cape Blanco". J. Amer. Irish Hist. Soc. 30:92-96.

Herlihy, D. J. 1951. Battle Against Bigotry: Father Yorke and the American Protective Association in San Francisco, 1893-1897. Records. Amer. Cath. Hist. Soc Philadelphia. 62:95-120.

Hogan, V. 1954. A Matchless Old Man. West Folklore 13:1-6.

Hitchman, R. and W. J. Wallrich. 1949. Names and Places. West, Folklore. 8:366-370.

Issel, W. 1977. Class and Ethnic Conflict in San Francisco Political History: The Reform Charter of 1898. Labor Hist. 18:341-359.

Jackson, W. T. 1959. The Irish Fox and the British Lion. Montana. 9:2:28-42.

Jones, I. 1956. Don Timoteo. Westways. 48:3:14-15.

Kilkenny, J. F. 1968. Shamrocks, and Shepherds: The Irish of Morrow County. Oregon Hist. Quart. 69:101-147.

_____. 1974. Alpine - A School to Remember. Oregon Hist. Quart. 75:270-276.

Knight, R. E. L. 1960. Industrial Relations in the San Francisco Bay Area 1900-1918. University of California, Berkeley.

Kunth, P. F. 1947. Nativism in California. Univ. of California, Berkeley. Masters thesis.

Lotchin, R. W. 1978. John Francis Neylan: San Francisco Irish Progressive. In: The Irish in San Francisco. J. P. Walsh, ed. Irish Liter. and Hist. Soc., San Francisco. pp. 87-110.

MacGowan, M. 1962. The Hard Road the Klondike. Routledge and Kegan Paul, London.

McGinty, B. 1978. The Green and the Gold. American West. 15:18-21, 65, 69.

Moloney, M. T. 1909. The Irish Pioneers of the West and Their Descendants. J. Amer. Irish Hist. Soc. 8:209-216.

O'Connor, R. C. 1916. The Irish in California. J. Amer. Irish Hist. Soc. 15:201-211.

O'Keane, J. 1955. Thomas J. Walsh: A Senator from Montana. M. Jones Co., Francestown, New Hampshire.

Prendergast, T. F. 1942. Forgotten Pioneers: Irish Leaders in Early California. The Trade Press-room, San Francisco.

Quigley, H. 1878. The Irish Race in California and on the Pacific Coast. A. Roman and Co., San Francisco.

Riordan, J. 1978. Garrett McEnerney and the Pursuit of Success. In: The Irish in San Francisco. J. P. Walsh, ed. Irish Liter. and Hist. Society, San Francisco. pp. 73-84.

Rooney, F. 1931. Irish Rebel and California Labor Leader: An Autobiography. Ed. by I. B. Cross. Univ. of California Press, Berkeley.

Starr, K. 1978. Jerry Brown: The Governor as Zen Jesuit. In: The San Francisco Irish. J. P. Walsh, ed. Irish Liter. and Hist. Soc., San Francisco. pp. 127-140.

Shumsky, N. L. 1976. Frank Roney's San Francisco -- His Diary: April, 1975 - March, 1976. Labor Hist. 17:2:245-264.

Walsh, J. P. 1971. American-Irish: West and East. Eire-Ireland. 6:2:25-32.

_____. 1973. Father Peter Yorke of San Francisco. Studies: An Irish Quart. Rev. 62:245:19-34.

_____. 1975. Peter Yorke and Progressivism in California, 1908. Eire, 10:2:73-80.

_____. 1978. Machine Politics, Reform and San Francisco. In: The Irish in San Francisco. J. P. Walsh, ed. Irish Liter. and Hist. Soc. pp. 59-72.

_____. 1978. Peter C. Yorke: San Francisco's Irishman Reconsidered. In: The San Francisco Irish. J. P. Walsh, ed. Irish Liter. and Hist. Soc., San Francisco. pp. 43-57.

_____. 1978. The Irish in Early San Francisco. In: The Irish in San Francisco. J. P. Walsh, ed. Irish Liter. Hist. Soc., San Francisco. pp. 9-25.

_____. 1978. The San Francisco Irish, 1850-1876. The Irish Literary and Historical Society, San Francisco.

SUPPLEMENT NO. 1:  BY TOPIC

## General Works on the Irish in America

Appel, J. C.  1950.  Immigrant Historical Societies
in the United States 1880-1950.  University of
Pennsylvania, Ph.D. dissertation.

Blessing, P. J.  1980.  Irish.  In: Harvard Encyclopedia of American Ethnic Groups.  S. Thernstrom
ed., Belknap Press, Cambridge, Massachusetts,
pp. 525-545.

Doyle, D. N.  1980.  America and Ireland 1776-1976.
The American Identity and the Irish Connection.
Greenwood Press, Westport, Connecticut.

_____.  1981.  Irish America, 1830-1940:  A
Regional Bibliography.  Irish Historical Studies
(in press).

Dwyer, T. R.  1974.  Americans and the Great Famine:
A Story of Human Concern.  Capuchin Ann. 1974:70-78.

Farley, J.  1965.  To Those of My Ancestry.  Friar,
23:3:46-49.

Greeley, A. M.  1980.  The Irish Americans:  The
Rise to Money and Power.  Times Books, New York.

Merwin, H. C.  1896.  The Irish in American Life.
Atlantic Monthly, 77:289-301.

Mitchell, A. H.  1969.  A View of the Irish in
America:  1887.  Eire-Ireland, 4:1:7-12.

O'Brien, M. J.  1914.  The Irish in the United States.
In:  The Glories of Ireland.  J. Dunn and P. J.
Lennox, eds.  Phoenix Ltd.  Washington, D.C., pp.
184-220.

O'Shea, J. J.  1899.  The Irish Leaven in American
Progress.  Forum, 27:285-296.

Sands, W. F. 1931. Irish in America. Fort. Rev. 38:199-202 (Reply: 38:219-221, Rej. 38:247-249).

Sheridan, P. B. 1977. The Protestant Irish Heritage in America. Library of Congress Research Service. Washington, D.C.

Smith, J. T. 1902. The Irish in the United States. Irish. Eccles. Rec. 4th Series, 11:532-44.

## The Irish Migration to America

Dillon, M. F. 1940. Irish Emigration, 1840-1855. U.C.L.A., Ph.D. dissertation.

Nolan, N. 1935. The Irish Emigration: A Study in Demography. University College Dublin, Ph.D. dissertation.

O'Brien, G. 1946. The Irish in America: Melting Pot. Studies: An Irish Quart. Rev., 35:343-350.

O'Grada, C. 1975. A Note on Nineteenth Century Irish Emigration Statistics. Pop. Stud. 29:143-149.

_____. 1980. Irish Emigration to the United States in the Nineteenth Century. In: America and Ireland 1776-1976. D. N. Doyle and O. D. Edwards, eds. Greenwood Press, Westport, New York, pp. 93-103.

Vedder, R. K. and L. E. Galloway. 1972. The Geographic Distribution of British and Irish Emigrants to the U.S. After 1800. Scottish J. Polit. Econ. 19:19-35.

Walsh, E. J. 1959. Language Problem of Irish Immigrants at the Time of the Famine. St. Meinrads Essays, 12:60-73.

## Socioeconomic Status and Mobility of the Irish in America

Dolin, M. C. 1925. American Irish Women Firsts. J. Amer. Irish Hist. Soc., 24:215-221.

Egelman, W. S. 1979. The Debate Over Ethnicity, 1900-1924: A Sociocultural Analysis. Ph.D. Fordham University.

Ehrlich, R. L. ed. 1977. Immigrants in Industrial America. 1850-1920. Univ. Virginia, Charlottesville.

Glad, D. C. 1947. Attitudes and Experiences of American-Jewish and American-Irish Male Youth as Related to Differences in Adult Rates of Inebriety. Quart. J. Stud. on Alcohol, 8:406-72.

Gerber, D. 1980. Ethnics, Enterprise and Middle Class Formation: Using the Dun and Bradstreet Collection for Research in Ethnic History. Immig. Hist. Newsletter, 12:1:1-7.

Greeley, A. M. and W. C. McCready. 1972. An Ethnic Group Which Vanished: The Strange Case of the American Irish. Soc. Stud., 1:1:38-50.

Greeley, A. M. 1977. An Ugly Little Secret Anti-Catholicism in North America. Sheed, Andrews and McMeel, Shawnee, Kansas.

_____. 1980. The American Achievement: A Report From Great Ireland. In: America and Ireland 1776-1976. D. N. Doyle and O. D. Edwards, eds. Greenwood Press, Westport, New York, pp. 232-246.

_____. et al. 1980. Ethnic Drinking Subcultures. Praeger, New York.

Griffen, C. 1977. The Old Immigration and Industrialization. In: Immigrants in Industrial America 1850-1920. R. L. Ehrlich, ed. Univ. Virginia, Charlottesville, pp. 176-204.

Katzman, D. M. 1978. Seven Days a Week: Women and Domestic Service in Industrializing America. Oxford Univ. Press, New York.

Knupfer, G. and R. Room. 1967. Drinking Patterns and Attitudes of Irish, Jewish and White Protestant American Men. Quart. J. Stud. on Alcohol, 28:676-699.

McCready, W. C. 1980. The Irish Neighborhood. In: America and Ireland 1776-1976. D. N. Doyle and O. D. Edwards, eds. Greenwood Press, Westport, New York, pp. 247-259.

McGarry, M. B. 1979. Modernism in the United States: William Lawrence Sullivan, 1872-1935. Rec. Amer. Cath. Hist. Soc. Philadelphia, 90:33-52.

McGouldrick, P. F. and M. B. Tanner. 1977. Did American Manufacturers Discriminate Against Immigrants Before 1914. J. Econ. Hist., 37:723-46.

Meehan, T. F. 1900. Archbishop Hughes and the Draft Riots. U.S. Cath. Hist. Soc. Hist. Rec. and Stud. I: 171-190.

Murphy, J. C. 1940. Attitudes of American Catholics Toward the Immigrant and the Negro. Catholic University, Masters Thesis.

Rice, M. H. 1944. American Catholic Opinion and the Anti-Slavery Controversy. Columbia Univ., New York.

Shapiro, C. 1980. Immigration: No Irish Need Apply. Ais-Eiri, 3:2:8-11.

Soloman, B. M. 1952. Background of Immigration Restriction. New Eng. Quart., 25:45-59.

## Irish-Americans and the Labor Movement

Doyle, D. N. 1975. The Irish and American Labor 1880-1920. Saothar: J. Irish Labor Hist. Soc., 1:42-53.

Doherty, R. E. 1962. Thomas O. Hagerty, The Church and Socialism. Labor Hist., 3:39-56.

Flaherty, W. B. 1970. The Clergyman and Labor Progress: Cornelius O'Leary and the Knights of Labor. Labor Hist. 11:175-189.

Flynn, E. G. 1955. I Speak My Own Piece: An Autobiography of the Rebel Girl. Masses and Mainstream, New York. (Reissued 1973, International Publ.).

Gutman, H. G. 1976. Class, Status and Community Power in Nineteenth Century American Industrial Cities: Paterson, New Jersey: A Case Study. In: Work, Culture and Society. H. G. Gutman. Alfred Knopf, New York, pp. 234-292.

Hirsch, S. E. 1978. Roots of the American Working Class: The Industrialization of Crafts in Newark 1800-1860. Univ. Penna. Press, Philadelphia.

Katzman, D. M. 1978. Seven Days a Week: Women and Domestic Service in Industrializing America. Oxford Univ., New York.

Montgomery, D. 1980. The Irish and the American Labor Movement. In: America and Ireland, 1776-1976. D. N. Doyle and O. D. Edwards, eds. Greenwood Press, Westport, New York, pp. 205-218.

O'Donnell, L. A. 1978. The Greening of a Limerick Man: Patrick Henry McCarthy. Eire/Ireland, 11:2: 119-128.

Scholten, P. C. 1979. The Old Mother and Her Army: The Agitative Strategies of Mary Harris Jones. W. Va. Hist. 40:4:365-374.

Wilentz, R. S. 1979. Industrializing America and the Irish: Towards the New Departure. Labor Hist. 20:4:579-595.

## The Irish-American in Politics

Beunker, J. D. 1971. The Mahatma and Progressive Reform: Martin Lomasney as Lawmaker, 1911-1917. New Eng. Quart. 44:397-419.

Bradley, H. C. 1966. Frank P. Walsh and Post War America. St. Louis Univ. Ph.D. dissertation.

Brown, T. N. 1980. The Political Irish: Politicians and Rebels. In: America and Ireland 1776-1976. D. N. Doyle and O. D. Edwards, eds. Greenwood Press, Westport, New York, pp. 133-149.

Cohalan, D. F. 1930. Andrew Jackson. J. Amer. Irish. Hist. Soc., 28:173-187.

Connor, C. P. 1979. The American Catholic Political Position at Mid-Century: Archbishop Hughes as a Test Case. Fordham Univ. Ph.D. dissertation.

Dinnerstein, L. 1961. The Impact of Tammany Hall on State and National Politics in the Eighteen-Eighties. New York Hist, 42:237-252.

Eisinger, P. K. 1980. Transition to Irish Rule in Boston, 1884-1933: A Case Study. In: The Politics of Development. P. K. Eisinger. Academic Press, New York, pp. 29-54.

Foster, M. 1968. Frank Hague of Jersey City: The Boss Reformer. New Jersey Hist., 85:106-117.

Gouldrick, J. W. 1979. John A. Ryans Theory of the State. Catholic Univ. Ph.D. dissertation.

Goldberg, J. S. 1979. Patrick Egan Irish-American Minister to Chile. Eire/Ireland, 14:3:83-95.

Greeley, A. M. 1974. Political Participation Among American Ethnic Groups in the U.S.: A Preliminary Reconnaisance. Amer. J. Socio. 80:170-204.

Greeley, A. M. 1975. A Model for Ethnic Political Socialization. Amer. J. Pol. Sci., 19:187-206.

Griffith, R. 1971. The Political Context of McCarthyism. Rev. Polit., 33:1:24-35.

Gudelunas, W. and S. R. Couch. 1980. Would a Protestant or Polish Kennedy Have Won?: A Local Test of Ethnicity and Religion in the Presidential Election of 1960. Ethnic Groups, 3:1-21.

Hanna, M. T. 1979. Catholics and American Politics. Harvard Univ. Cambridge, Mass.

Kelly, R. 1977. Ideology and Political Culture Jefferson to Nixon. Amer. Hist. Rev., 82:531-582.

Kennedy, J. H. 1930. Governor Dongar and Religious Liberty in New York, 1683-1688. J. Amer. Irish Hist. Soc., 28:100-106.

Kenneally, J. 1980. Prelude to the Last Hurrah: Massachusetts Senatorial Election of 1936. Mid-Amer., 62:1:3-20.

O'Brien, M. 1980. Young Joe McCarthy, 1908-1944. Wis. Mags. Hist., 63:179-323.

O'Connor, R. 1970. The First Hurrah: A Biography of Alfred E. Smith. Putnam, New York.

O'Hare, J. D. 1959. The Public Career of Patrick Andrew Collins. Boston Col. Ph.D. dissertation.

Rakove, M. 1980. Jane Byrne and the New Chicago Politics. Chicago Political Series. Center for Urban Affairs Northwestern Univ. Evanston, Illinois.

Senkewicz, R. M. 1979. Religion and Non-Partisan Politics in the Gold Rush, San Francisco. Southern California Quart., 61:351-378.

Shaw, D. V. 1977. Political Leadership in an Industrial City: Irish Development and Nativist Response in Jersey City. In: Immigrants in Industrial America 1850-1920. R. L. Ehrlich, ed. Univ. of Virginia, Charlottesville, pp. 85-95.

Weiss, R. 1979. Ethnicity and Reform: Minorities and the Ambience of the Depression Years. J. Amer. Hist., 66:566-585,

## Irish-Americans at War

Brennan, T. 1976, Brennans and Brannans in American Military and Naval Life 1745-1810. Irish Sword, 12: 48:239-245.

Burton, W. L. 1980. "Title Deed to America" Union Ethnic Regiments in the Civil War. Proc. Amer. Philos. Soc., 124:6:455-463.

Calkin, H. 1957. James Leander Cathcart and the U.S. Navy. Irish Sword, 3:145-58.

Costello, J. J. 1980. The Irish and the American Military Tradition. In: America and Ireland, 1776-1976. D. N. Doyle and O. D. Edwards, eds. Greenwood Press, Westport, New York, pp. 219-228.

Doyle, D. N. 1979. Irishmen and Revolutionary America, 1740-1820. Mercer, Cork.

Fawcus, S. E. 1971. The Irish in America and the Struggle for Irish Independence. Bryn Mawr College, Masters Thesis.

Galway, T. F. 1961. The Valiant Hours. Stackpole Co. Harrisburg, Pennsylvania.

Hassler, W. W. 1979. The Irrepressible James Shields Lincoln Herald, 81:3:187-191.

McAvoy, T. T. 1932, Peter Paul Cooney. J. Amer. Irish Hist. Soc., 30:97-102.

McEnroy, B. M. 1937. American Catholics and War with Mexico. Washington, D.C.

Mitchell, A. H. 1977. Irishmen and the American Revolution. Capuchin Annual, 1977:70-88.

206

Monaghan, F. 1930. Stephan Moylan in the American Revolution. Studies: An Irish Quart., 19:481-486.

Murphy, W. S. 1962. Four Soldiers of the American Revolution. Irish Sword, 5:164-174.

_____. 1963. Four American Officers of the War of 1812. Irish Sword, 6:1-12.

O'Flaherty, P. D. 1963. The History of the Fighting Sixty-Ninth Regiment of the New York State Militia, 1852-1861. Fordham Univ. Ph.D. dissertation.

O'Snodaigh, P. 1970. Eirenaigh Sa Chogadh Chathartha Sna Strait Aontaithe. Studia Hibernica, 16:95-107 (Irish in the Civil War).

White, C. M. 1979. Charles Thomson: The Irish-Born Sect of the Cont. Congress 1774-1789. Studies: Irish Quart., 68:269-270:33-45.

Irish-America and Irish Nationalism

Bisceglia, L. R. 1981. The McManus Welcome, San Francisco, 1851. Eire/Ireland, 16:1:6-20.

Fleming, T. 1979. The Green Flag in America. Amer. Heritage, 30:4:50-63.

Murphy, J. H. 1980. The Influence of America on Irish Nationalism. In: America and Ireland 1776-1976. D. N. Doyle and O. D. Edwards, eds. O'Sullivan, S. 1977. A Similarity in Our Causes. Eire/Ireland, 12:4:6-24.

Reidy, J. 1928. John Devoy. J. Amer. Irish Hist. Soc., 27:413-425.

Rosen, R. 1979. The Catalpa Rescue. J. Roy. Austral. Hist. Soc., 65:2:73-88.

Stockley, W. F. P. 1935. Reminiscences of John Boyle O'Reilly 1844-1890. Cath. World, 140:664-72, 141:73-81.

# Irish-American Religion and the Catholic Church

Alvarez, D. J., ed. 1979. An American Church. St. Mary's College, Moraga, California.

Anon. 1881. Irish Faith in America: Recollections of a Missionary. New York. (Translated Ella McMahon)

Blessing, P. 1980. Culture, Religion and the Activities of the Committee of Vigilance, San Francisco 1850. Amer. Cath. Stud. Seminar. Univ. of Notre Dame, November, 1980.

Coogan, M. J. 1980. The Redoubtable John Hennesey First Archbishop of Dubuque. Mid-America, 62-21-34.

Curley, M. J. 1958. Deeper Study of Catholic Immigration Needed. Rec. Amer. Cath. Hist. Soc. 69:56-62.

_____. 1968. The Catholic Experience - Another View. Rec. Amer. Cath. Hist. Soc. 79:39-49.

Deedy, J. 1978. Seven American Catholics. Thomas More Assn. Chicago.

Doyle, D. N. 1980. The Irish and the Christian Churches in America. In: America and Ireland 1776-1976. D. N. Doyle and O. D. Edwards, eds. Greenwood Press, Westport, New York. pp. 177-191.

Gleason, P. 1959. Not German or Irish, So Much as Catholics. Social Justice Review. 51:384-385.

Grozier, R. J. 1966. The Life and Times of John Bernard Fitzpatrick Third Roman Catholic Bishop of Boston, Boston Univ., Ph.D. dissertation.

Guilday, P. K. 1922. Life and Times of John Carroll. Archbishop of Baltimore. Encyclopedia, New York.

Gwynn, A. 1932. First Irish Priests in the New World. Studies: An Irish Quart. Rev., 21:213-228.

Hennesey, J. 1966. Papacy and Episcopacy in Nineteenth Century America. Rec. Amer. Cath. Hist. Soc., 77:175-189.

Leslie, S. 1918. Lost Irish in the U.S.A.: The Church in the Deep South. Tablet, 211:103-104.

Manfra, J. 1975. The Catholic Episopacy in America, 1789-1852. University of Iowa, Ph.D. dissertation.

Maynard, T. 1941. How American Catholicism was Cast in an Urban World. Commonwealth, 34:533-36.

McKeown, E. 1980. The National Bishops Conference: An Analysis of Its Origins. Cath. Hist. Rev., 66: 4:565-583.

McNamara, R. F. 1979. Bernard J. McQuaid's Sermon on Theological "Americanism." Rec. Amer. Cath. Hist. Soc. Phila., 90:23-32.

Miller, R. M. 1981. A Church in Cultural Captivity: Some Speculations on Catholic Identity in the Old South. Amer. Cath. Studies Seminar, Univ. of Notre Dame, Notre Dame, Indiana, February 14, 1981.

Nary, R. 1967. Church, State and Religious Liberty: Views of the American Catholic Bishops of the 1890's. Georgetown Univ., Ph.D. dissertation.

Purcell, R. J. 1942. Missionaries From All Hallows to the United States, 1842-1865. Amer. Cath. Hist. Soc. Rec.. 53:204-259.

Rodechko, J. P. 1970. An Irish-American Journalist and Catholicism: Patrick Food of the Irish World. Church Hist., 39:524-540.

Savard, P. 1971. Relations Between French Canadians and American Catholics in the Last Third of the 19th Century. Culture, 31:24-39.

Schmandt, R. H. 1979. Notes Toward a Biography of Archbishop Patrick J. Ryan. Rec. Amer. Cath. Hist. Soc. Phila., 90:69-84.

Sheerin, J. 1975. Never Look Back: Biography of John J. Burke. Paulist Press, New York.

Shinnors, M. F. 1902. Ireland and America: Some Notes of a Mission Tour in the United States. Irish Eccles. Rec., 4th Series, 11:114-126, 485-99.

Wakin, E. 1976. Catholic Like No Other: The Collective Achievement of the American Irish. Sign 56:18-22.

_____. 1976. You May Search Everywhere But None Can Compare: Irish Catholics in the U.S. U.S. Catholic, 41:7:35-39.

Williams, P. W. 1980. Catholicism Militant: The Public Face of the Archdiocese of Cincinnati, 1900-1960. Amer. Cath. Studies Seminar, Univ. Notre Dame, October, 1980.

Wangler, T. E. 1968. The Ecclesiology of Archbishop John Ireland: Its Nature, Development and Influence. Marquette Univ. Ph.D. dissertation.

Weber, F. J. 1968. Thomas McAvoy, CSC. Historian of American Catholicism. Ind. Mags. Hist., 64:15-24.

## The Scotch-Irish - Myth or Reality

Jones, M. D. 1980. Scotch-Irish. In: Harvard Encyclopedia of American Ethnic Groups. S. Thernstrom, ed. Belknap Press, Cambridge, Mass., pp. 896-908.

Klein, M. 1979. A Race in Upheaval. Part I. Amer. Hist. Illust., 13:9:30-38.

_____. 1979. The Nation Builders. Part II. Amer. Hist. Illust., 13:10:32-39.

_____. 1980. The Nation Builders. Part III. Amer. Hist. Illust., 14:1:8-12, 15-17.

Marshall, W. F. 1943. Ulster Sails West. Quota Press, Belfast, Ireland.

## The Irish in Canada

Anon. 1930. The Benevolent Irish Society. St. Johns, Newfoundland. J. Amer. Irish Hist. Soc., 28:155-156.

Burke, N. R. 1971. Some Observations on the migration of labourers from the south of Ireland to Newfoundland in pre-faminine times. Cork. Hist. Arch. Soc. J., 76:95-109.

Burley, K. 1978. Occupational Structure and Ethnicity in London, Ontario 1871. Historic Sociale - Social History, 11:22:390-410.

Brannigan, C. J. 1977. The Luke Dillon Case and the Welland Canal Explosion of 1900. Niagra Frontier, 24:2:36-44.

Browne, P. W. 1931. Irish Bishops in Newfoundland (1794-1893). Studies: An Irish Quart. Rev., 20: 49-66.

_____. 1933. Fateful 47. Ave Marie, 37:403-404.

_____. 1933. Noteworthy Centennial. Irish Eccl. Rec. 5th Series, 42:11-19.

_____. 1934. Aftermath of 47. Irish Monthly, 62:613-621.

Cushing, J. et al. 1979. A Chronicle of Irish Emigration to St. John, New Brunswick 1847. New Brunswick Museum, New Brunswick, Canada.

Darroch, A. G. and M. D. Ornstein. 1980. Ethnicity and Occupational Structure in Canada in 1871: A Vertical Mosaic in Historical Perspective. Can. Hist. Rev., 61:3:305-333.

Duggan, G. C. 1967. The Fenians in Canada: A British Officer's Impression. Irish Sword, 8:31: 88-91.

Forde, F. 1967. The Irish Regiment of Canada. Irish Defense J., 27:489-493.

Foster, F. G. 1979. Irish in Avalon: A Study of the Gaelic Language in Eastern Newfoundland. Aspects, 10:2:17-22.

Fox, R. W. 1977. Modernizing Mobility Studies. Hist. Educ. Quart., 17:2:203-209.

Gagan, D. 1978. Land, Population and Social Change: The Critical Years in Rural Canada. West. Can. Hist. Rev., 59:3:293-318.

Gagan, D. and H. Mays. 1973. Historical Demography and Canadian Social History: Families and Land in Peel County, Ontario. Can. Hist. Rev., 14:1:27-47.

Hennessy, M. F. ed. 1979. The Catholic Church in Prince Edward Island. 1720-1979. Roman Catholic Episcopal Corp., Charlottestown.

Houston, C. J. and W. J. Smyth. 1980. The Sash Canada Wore: A Historical Geography of the Orange Order in Canada. Univ. Toronto. Toronto, Canada.

Kelly, E. T. 1969. A Bridge of Fish: The Irish Connection with Newfoundland 1500-1630. Eire-Ireland, 4:2:37-51.

LaBranche, B. 1975. The Peter Robinson Settlement of 1825. Homecoming 75 Committee. Peterborough, Ontario.

Lee-Whiting, B. 1979. Chored Around All Day. Beaver, 310:1:12-16.

Lyne, D. C. 1967. Irish-Canadian Financial Con-tributions to the Home Rule Movement in the 1890's. Stud. Hib., 7:182-206.

Lyne, D. C. and P. M. Toner. 1972. Feninianism in Canada 1874-84. Studies Hibernia, 12:27-76.

MacKenzie, A. A. 1979. The Irish in Cape Breton. Formac, Antigonish, Nova Scotia.

Mannion, J. 1973. The Irish Migrations to New-foundland. Newfoundland Hist. Soc. Lecture, 1-12.

Mannion, J. J. 1976. Point Lance in Transition: The Transformation of a Newfoundland Outpost. McClelland and Stewart, Toronto.

Millar, J. L. 1979. The Life and Times of James Boyle Uniache. Nova Scotia Hist. Quart., 9:3:225-233.

Morgan, R. J. 1969. Orphan Outpost: Cape Breton an Associate Colony. 1784-1820. Univ. of Ottawa. Ph.D. dissertation.

O'Cathaoir, B. 1967. American Fenianism and Canada, 1865-71. Irish Sword, 8:31:77-87.

O'Reilly, J. B. 1947. Irish Famine and Atlantic Migration to Canada. Irish Eccl. Rec. 5th Series, 69:870-882.

Perin, R. 1980. Troppo Ardenti Sacerdoti: The Conroy Mission Revisited. Can. Hist. Rev., 61:3: 283-304.

Press, E. C. 1978. The Irish: The Urban Ethnic. In: Banked Fires: The Ethnics of Nova Scotia. D. F. Campbell, eds. Scribblers Press. Port Credit, Ontario. pp. 93-112.

Punch, T. 1976. The Irish in Halifax, A Study in Ethnic Assimilation. Dalhousie Univ. Ph.D. dissertation.

Scott, J. 1974. Striking Irishmen on the Lachine Canal. In: Sweat and Struggle: Working Class Struggles in Canada. J. Scott. New Star Books, Vancouver. pp. 67-74.

Smyth, W. J. 1977. The Irish in Mid-Nineteenth Century Ontario. Ulster Folklife, 23:97-105.

Walsh, J. J. 1914. The Irish in Canada. In: The Gloves of Ireland. J. Dunn and P. J. Lennox, eds. Phoenix Ltd., Washington, D.C., pp. 221-227.

# The Irish in New England

Baum, D. 1980. The "Irish Vote" and Party Politics in Massachusetts, 1860-1876. Civil War Hist., 26: 117-141.

Blaine, J. G. III. 1978. The Birth of a Neighborhood: 19th Century Charlestown, Massachusetts. Univ. Michigan. Ph.D. dissertation.

Dublin, T. 1979. Women at Work: The Transformation of Work and Community in Lowell, Massachusetts 1826-1860. Columbia Univ., New York.

Earles, M. 1933. Old Ireland in New England. Monthly, 162:109-117.

Field, A. J. 1979. Economic and Demographic Determinants of Educational Committment, Massachusetts 1855. J. Econ. Hist., 39:2:439-459.

Kantrowitz, N. 1979. Racial and Ethnic Residential Segregation in Boston 1830-1970. Annals. Amer. Acad: Polit., 441:41-54.

Kenneally, J. J. 1979. The Burning of the Ursuline Convent: A Different View. Rec. Amer. Cath. Hist. Soc. Philadelphia, 90:15-21.

McCaffrey, L. 1976. Boston's Irish More to be Pitied Than Censored. Listening, 11:9:161-174.

Merwick, D. J. 1968. Changing Thought Patterns of Three Generations of Catholic Clergymen of the Boston Archdiocese from 1850-1910. Univ. Wisconsin. Ph.D. dissertation.

Quinlan, R. J. 1937. Growth and Development of Catholic Education in the Archdiocese of Boston. Cath. Hist. Rev., 22:27-41.

Silvia, P. T., Jr. 1973. The Spindle City, Labor Politics and Religion in Fall River 1870-1945. Fordham Univ. Ph.D. dissertation.

_____. 1979. The "Flint River" Affair: French-Canadian Struggle for Survivance. Cath. Hist. Rev., 65:3:414-435.

Whyte, W. F. 1939. Race Conflicts in the North End of Boston. New Eng. Quart., 12:623-642.


The Irish in New York and the Middle Atlantic States

Barnard, W. F. 1893. Forty Years at the Five Points. Five Points House of Industry, New York.

Bigelow, B. L. 1978. Ethnic Stratification in a Pedestrian City: A Social Geography of Syracuse, New York. Syracuse Univ. Ph.D. dissertation.

Burstein, A. N. 1975. Residential Distribution and Mobility of Irish and German Immigrants in Philadelphia, 1850-1880. Univ. Pennsylvania. Ph.D. dissertation.

Clark, D. 1973. Urban Blacks and Irishmen: Brothers in Prejudice. In: Black Politics in Philadelphia. M. Ershowitz and J. Zikmund II, eds. Basic Books, New York, pp. 15-30.

Clark, D. J. 1978. Ethnic Enterprise and Urban Development. Ethnicity, 5:2:108-118.

Cook, L. 1980. St. Patricks Cathedral: A Centennial History. Quick Fox, New York.

Cunningham, B. ed. 1977. The New Jersey Ethnic Experience. William H. Wise, Union City, New Jersey.

Donahue, J. 1962. Gaelic Benevolence. Amer. Cath. Hist. Soc. Rec., 74:67-69.

Grimes, M. R. 1974. Some Newspaper References to Irish Immigrants in Oneida County New York. Irish Ancestry: 6:2:97-98.

Haines, M. R. 1980. Fertility and Marriage in a Nineteenth Century Industrial City: Philadelphia, 1850-1880. J. Econ. Hist., 40:1:151-158.

Hershberg, T. et al., 1979. A Tale of Three Cities: Blacks and Immigrants in Philadelphia, 1850-1880, 1930 and 1970. Annals Amer. Acad. Polit. and Soc. Sci., 441:55-81.

Hickey, M. E. 1933. Irish Catholics in Washington up to 1860. Catholic Univ. Masters Thesis.

Hollingsworth, G. 1973. Irish Quakers in Colonial Pennsylvania: A Forgotten Segment of Society. J. Lancaster Co. Hist. Soc., 79:3:150-162.

Ralph, R. M. 1978. The City and the Church Catholic Beginnings in Newark 1840-70. New Jersey Hist., 96:3-4:105-118.

Turbin, C. 1979. And We Are Nothing But Women: Irish Working Women in Troy. In: Women of America. Berkin, C. R. and M. B. Norton, eds. Houghton Mifflin, Boston.

Van Denmark, H. 1930. Irish and Dutch in Old New York. America, 44:33-34.

## The Irish in the North Central States

Bartha, S. J. 1945. The Irish. In: A History of Immigrant Groups in Toledo. S. J. Bartha. Masters Thesis. Ohio State Univ. pp. 23-39.

Carey, S. H. 1944. The Irish Element in Iowa up to 1865. Catholic Univ. Masters Thesis.

Cudahy, P. 1912. Patrick Cudahy: His Life. Milwaukee. Burdick and Allen.

Deininger, M. and D. Marshall. 1955. A Study of Land Ownership by Ethnic Groups from Frontier Times to the Present in a Marginal Farming Area in Minnesota Land Economics, 31:351-360.

Duchschere, K. A. 1979. John Stanley: North Dakotas' First Catholic Bishop. No. Dak. Hist., 46:2:4-13.

Fanning, C, et al. 1980. Nineteenth Century Chicago Irish: A Social and Political Portrait. Loyola Univ., Chicago.

Fanning, C. and E. Skerrett. 1979. James T. Farrell and Washington Park: The Novel as Social History. Chicago History. Summer 1979:80-91.

Fanning, C. 1978. Finlay Peter Dunne and Mr. Dooley: The Chicago Years. University of Kentucky, Lexington.

Flanagan, K. D. 1971. A Cultural Interpretation of Occupational Trends Amongst Irish-Americans in Minnesota, 1870-1900. Univ. Minnesota. Masters Thesis.

Greeley, A. M. 1979. Looking Backward: Commodore Barry Country Club in Twin Lakes Wisconsin. Chicago Hist., 8:2:112-119.

Skerrett, E. 1981. The Irish Parish in Chicago, 1880-1930. Amer. Cath. Stud. Seminar, Univ. of Notre Dame. Notre Dame. March 7, 1981.

Zunz, O. 1977. The Organization of the American City in the Late Nineteenth Century: Ethnic Structure and Spatial Arrangement in Detroit. J. Urban Hist. 3:4:443-466.

## The Irish in the South and Southwest

Blessing, P. J. 1980. The British and Irish in Oklahoma. Univ. of Oklahoma, Norman.

Fitzmaurice, M. A. 1926. Four Decades of Catholicism in Texas, 1820-1860. Catholic Univ., Masters Thesis.

Flanigan, J. J. 1951. The Irish Element in Nashville, 1810-1890. Vanderbilt Univ., Masters Thesis.

Flannery, J. 1980. The Irish Texas. Tirawley Distributors, San Antonio, Texas.

Galloway, M. K. n.d. The Irish of Staggers Point. Manuscript on file, Library of Institute of Texas Cultures, San Antonio.

Gilbert, F. V. 1946. Georgia Irish Travellers Are A Race Apart. Cath. Digest, 10:20-21.

Harper, J. 1969. Irish Traveler Cant: A Historical, Structural and Sociolinguistic Study of an Argot. Univ. of Georgia. Masters Thesis.

Harper, J. 1971. "Gypsy" Research in the South. Southern Anthropological Society Proc., 4:16-24.

Harper, J. and C. Hudson. 1971. Irish Traveler Cant. J. Eng. Linguistics, 5-6:78-86.

Herbert, R. B. 1981. San Patricio de Hiberniae, the Forgotten Colony. Herbert, Texas.

Kearns, K. C. 1979. Population Shift and the Settlement Patterns of Irish Travellers. Irish. Geog., 11:23-34.

Leslie, S. 1958. Lost Irish the Church in the Deep South. Tablet, 211:103-104.

Linenan, J. C. 1899. The Irish Pioneers of Texas. J. Amer. Irish Hist. Soc., 2:124-26.

McBeath, J. J. 1953. The Irish Empressarios of Texas. Catholic Univ. Masters Thesis.

McDonald, F. 1978. The Ethnic Factor in Alabama History: A Neglected Dimension. Ala. Hist., 31:256-265.

McDonald, F. and E. S. McDonald. 1980. The Ethnic Origins of the American People, 1790. William and Mary Quart., 3rd Series, 37:179-199.

McDonald, F. and G. McWhiney. 1980. The Celtic South. History Today, 30:11-15.

McDonald, F. and G. McWhiney. 1975. The Antebellum Southern Herdsman: A Reinterpretation. J. Southern Hist., 41:147-166.

McNamee, J. 1975. Breaking the Crust of Custom. Tulsa, Oklahoma.

McWhiney, G. 1978. The Revolution in 19th Century Alabama Agriculture. Ala. Rev., 31:3-32.

Muller, E. 1941. Roving the South with the Irish Horse Traders. Readers Digest, 39:231:59-63.

Nordheimer, J. 1971. Irish Travellers Are A Race Apart. Cath. Digest, 35:3:86-88.

Price, W. 1950. People Who Hid for 200 Years: Appalachin Americans. Cath. Digest, 14:8:44-51.

Ryan, G. 1967. The Irish Travelers. Ave Maria, 105:3:16-18.

Smith, J. E. Jr. 1930. Thomas Burke, Governor of North Carolina. J. Amer. Irish Hist. Soc., 28:61-64.

Triga, L. 1940. Fr. Miguel Muldoon. St. Marys Univ., Texas, Masters Thesis.

Warburton, M. R. 1939. A History of the O'Connor Ranch 1834-1939. Catholic Univ., Masters Thesis.

## The Irish in the Farwest

Blessing, P. J. 1980. Culture, Religion and the Activities of the Committee of Vigilance, San Francisco, 1856. Center for the Study of American Catholicism. American Catholic Studies Seminar, November 1, 1980.

O'Donnell, L. A. 1979. From Limeric to the Golden Gate: Odyssey of an Irish Carpenter. Studies: An Irish Quart., 68:269-270:76-91.

Senkewicz, R. M. 1974. Business and Politics in Gold Rush San Francisco. Stanford Univ. Ph.D. dissertation.

_____. 1979. American and Catholic: The Premature Synthesis of the San Francisco Irish. In: An American Church, D. J. Alvarez, eds. St. Mary's College, Moraga, California, pp. 141-151.

Stack, R. E. 1972. The McCleers and the Birneys: Irish Immigrant Families Into Michigan and the Californian Gold Fields, 1820-1893. St. Louis Univ. Ph.D. dissertation.

Walsh, J. P. 1980. The Irish in the New America Way Out West. In: America and Ireland, 1776-1976. D. N. Doyle and O. D. Edwards, eds. Greenwood Press, Westport, New York, pp. 165-176.

Williams, D. A. 1969. David C. Broderick. Huntingdon Library, San Marino, California.

Wright, D. M. 1940. The Making of Cosmopolitan California: An Analysis of Immigration, 1848-1870. California Hist. Soc. Quart., 70:323-43.